...AND THE CATHEDRAL FELL TO THE GROUND

the lonesome death of rock & roll

MIKE DERRICO

Paperback ISBN: 978-1-7354767-4-2

eBook ISBN: 978-1-7354767-5-9

Cover & Interior formatting by Abbey Suchoski.

To Sal...

friend, brother, rock & roll guru

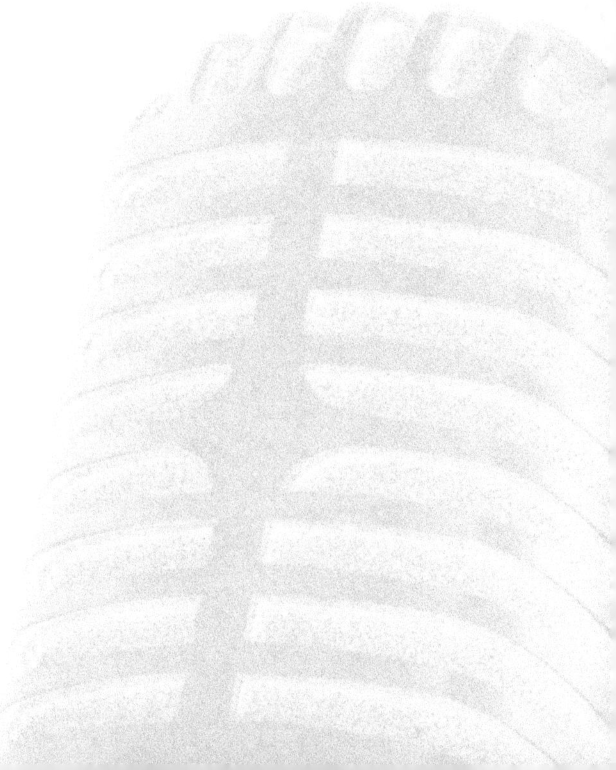

Contents

INTRODUCTION

As far back as I can remember, there has always existed the nay-saying mentality stating rock is dead. They had rock dead in the late 1950s, and then they had it dead in the late 1960s even as the first rock "revival" was getting underway. Pete Townshend had it dead in the middle of *Odds & Sods* in 1974. Then disco killed it. Then metal castrated and sterilized it by extracting every trace of the blues from it. Then it was supposedly born again in the coming of some bands from Seattle. Then Christ Kurt eliminated himself from the picture and his drummer ended up becoming far more influential over the next 20-plus years than Kurt could have ever been...which really negates the worn out idea that the short-lived popularity of what Bob Dylan called the celestial grunge didn't have much long-term impact past the mid-1990s...though many quickly began to attribute Kurt Cobain's death as the dividing line...and the official end of what Casey Kasem referred to as the "rock era." We say dividing line because while many believe rock has died a thousand deaths over the years, it is not always wise to suggest rock just abruptly ended in 1994. What becomes more plausible is if we suggest that while rock has continued in color-by-numbers/connect the dots form in the decades since,

1994 becomes a good pinpoint area of focus when we assess the end of rock as the center of the pop cultural zeitgeist and the beginning of rock being primarily associated with "grandparent music," "legacy acts," and anything that future generations would hold in a negative, joking and dismissive light as something for old white people. Musical taxonomists would soon resort to calling the music on the earlier side of this line "classic rock," while it inescapably unfolds as the last generation of culturally relevant rock with respect to the big picture, and though I myself am not making any concrete claim that rock is officially dead, I'm putting forth stationary examples as evidence that rock as we once knew it was extinguished a long time ago. This is all well and good to the larger point of this book, but for the time being, let me stay focused on age and two other facts...one, that time waits for no one...and two, that our rock icons are dropping at a rate like we never imagined. They're no longer dying prematurely at the age of 27. The ones who made it and went the distance are now expiring in twos and threes. The prospects of a world with no living Beatles or Rolling Stones become more real with each passing year. When I started this book, Charlie Watts was still with us. Now he's not. God only knows at this point who else will be missing by the time I can publish this.

The major revelation for me upon turning 50 under lockdown was the realization that my main creative goal in life now is to publish as many books as I can...and that the massive magnum opus I'm working on with 2025/26 in mind is by far the biggest thing I've ever attempted... so it's a good idea if that's the one that attracts a real publisher that can actually do me some good. In the meantime, I've taken the indie route after years of hesitation, which allowed me the chance to put my first two books out in 2020 and 2021. Whether that's valid enough for some no longer concerns me. I've learned the hard way that the approval we seek the most sometimes never comes in this lifetime. And when you've gone so long without the opportunity to thrive, it becomes necessary to create your own environment to thrive, whether successful in someone else's eyes or not. At that point, it becomes a necessity for your own survival. Regarding that magnum opus, this particular book is an aside and will unquestionably come out long before that much bigger book.

What this particular book is, is a small collection of what I call opinionated vignettes (sort of) through a recollection of memories and instances, both personal and cultural, where the underlying struggle and end result was some kind of change to an otherwise perfect system of familiarity...one that we thought as kids would last forever. But everything we ever know to be concrete and permanent crumbles to shit. We get old. We get crotchety, unforgiving and resentful. Too many for comfort turn conservative and end up lamenting the unraveling and eventual loss of what we unavoidably know as the "good old days." We say things like "That's when music was music...that's when baseball was baseball...that's when food was food"...stupid things like that. The "good old days" conversations don't begin when we're old. They begin when we're still young. Teenagers get sentimental for early childhood. Kids in their twenties get sentimental for their entire childhoods. Adults in their thirties and forties get sentimental for high school. Adults in their fifties get sentimental for their twenties and thirties. It's a never ending circle of looking back. But through it all...at least in my time...which begins in 1970...one of the ever-present common threads of resentful bickering has been the sentiment that rock music is dead.

So when did it die? If it died, then when did it happen? Was it old age? Was it violent? Was it murdered? Was it a slow decline? Was someone responsible? Was it something that happened over time? It must have been, because every generation has said the same thing. Yet, going into the second and third decades of the twenty-first century, something started to feel rather permanent with respect to rock's disappearance from the mainstream zeitgeist. What changes happened? Were they major changes that had significance to the overall big picture of pop culture? Or were they changes in our own personal lives that mimicked cultural changes, thus creating the illusion of entire eras ending when in fact they still remained intact? There are kids out there having rock experiences that are just as real as anything that's ever been. So, where do we find these changes if they weren't all personal? They told us rock and roll would never die. It would always be. When did the first cracks in the foundation appear? How and when did they progress? We can all answer these questions in our own book addressing this topic if we wanted to. Anyone can write their own version of this book. So to claim my takes in the following pages as the answer to anything would be useless and just plain stupid. All of these personal experiences of music I've recounted in these pages simply convey the joy of living far more than it could ever be a joy of living *without* the music. Each and every one of them contain a situation where there is an elemental passion for something we were told would never die. They all happened during a time when we thought that to be true. And what also underlies these recollections are accompanying experiences of change...moments when we realized our version of pop culture as well as how we looked at our own lives was finite, and that our ideas of forever were merely fragile constructions of the human intellect. We've all had our own personal encounters with the cracks in the foundation. These are mine.

"Something moved, it's out there."

– Tod Howarth

1

THE NIGHT I WAS SHOT AT WHITE CASTLE AND DIED IN THE SHOWER

At some point in my mid twenties, it occurred to me that one day I would officially outlive all of those dead rock stars who died at the age of 27. It seemed surreal. When I got as old as 25 or 26, artists like Jimi Hendrix still seemed so worldly and evolved, as if they had passed through far more lives than I ever would have passed through by that same age. But on May 9, 1998, I turned 28, and it hit me that I had been alive longer than Hendrix was. And Janis Joplin, and Brian Jones, and Otis Redding, and Jim Morrison, and Kurt Cobain. I politely include Kurt in this only because he died at 27. I did not grow up listening to Kurt's music the way I did the others, simply because he was only three years older than me, and we were pretty much the same generation. But there are rock stars of all ages that have died. This same profound thought has materialized every time I realize I've outlived someone. When I turned 33, I realized I outlived Keith Moon and John Bonham, and that's not even the surprising part considering that I myself didn't think I would live to see thirty. In my mid-twenties, I contracted a scary case of mono followed by months and months of debilitating chronic fatigue syndrome. Two years later, I got hit with some intestinal issues coupled with pneumonia and ended up undergoing entire batteries of testing which showed nothing serious...but the psychological damage was already long done, as those few years created decades of anxiety, hypochondria and a fixation on death. Long story short, I got over all of that, but the point I'm making here is that I could probably come up with a noteworthy death for every year of my adult life where I've realized I've outlived yet another rock artist...and man, it's strange to know you've been on the planet longer than your icons were.

When I turned forty, I immediately calculated the time frame between John Lennon's fortieth birthday and his death. Lennon lived only 60 days past turning forty. With that information applied to myself and imagining myself as Lennon, I did the math and tabulated my death day as July 8, 2010. I remember a few days before July 8, thinking *Damn, if I were John Lennon I'd only have a few days to live.*

July 8, 2010

It's around 8:15 PM and I don't have anything in particular to do tonight. The sky is flirting with twilight as I sit on the back deck, watching some friends playing horseshoes. I hate horseshoes and would usually rather undergo a root canal than watching drunkards on a weeknight tossing a bunch of cast iron across the ground, clanking away while bragging about whose drug tolerance is higher and pissing off the neighbors. At some point, I leave and take a lengthy drive somewhere. I'm on the road as it grows dark. After an hour or so, I realize how hungry I am, not having had dinner, so I end up in a dreadfully long White Castle drive-thru line. I glance at the dashboard and the clock reads 10:40-something as I approach the point of ordering. I sit there thinking to myself...

If I were John Lennon, I'd be getting out of the limo right about now. I'll be shot in another minute.

As I'm thinking this, I'm interrupted by a woman named Paula who cuts through a speaker at the top of the drive thru menu and says in one breath, "GoodeveningwelcometoWhiteCastlemy nameisPaula-mayItakeyourorder?"

As I'm flashing on Lennon walking past the guard booth toward his bloody death, Paula wants to know what I want to eat.

"I'll have a number one with a Coke please," I tell her.

Lennon is shot four times. The sound rings out and echoes across West Seventy-Second Street, up and down Central Park West and beyond.

"Would you like that with cheese or without?"

Lennon stumbles up six stairs and enters the security office where guard Jay Hastings is situated and Yoko is now passing through, having entered first, about 30 steps ahead of John. Startled by the shots, Yoko stops in the office and is horrified to see her husband burst through the door and collapse face down on the floor. She shrieks out a blood-curdling scream and collapses to her knees over his body, his glasses knocked off his face...the same bloody glasses that would soon be imposed on the retina of the world some six months later when they appear on the cover of Yoko's *Season of Glass* album.

"With cheese. And can I get one bacon and cheddar slider in addition to that?"

My mom tells me that I danced with the refrigerator to "Maggie May" at the age of one. I have no memory of this, but as the story goes, I was just learning how to walk...and when the Rod Stewart classic (brand new at the time) would come on the radio, I'd stand with my hands against the green Frigidaire and sway back and forth from leg to leg. I suppose this was the first music I was affected by.

Slightly off topic but always crucial to the point, I'm one of those people with Superior Autobiographical Memory. These are the people who can literally remember every day of their lives. You can throw any random date at them and they'll tell you what they did that day... what they wore, what they ate, where they went, what day of the week it was and minute details like that. Anyway, I'm sort of one of those people. *Sort of* meaning there are less than 50 confirmed cases around the world, and I'm not officially one of them, as I only have a mild case of it and I'm not nearly as endowed in the minutia of memory as the most severe cases. Most memories I have though, are accompanied by music. Memories and music seem to go hand-in-hand throughout our lives. This can be said of most people, although many are not aware of it, and many who are aware don't spend too much time contemplating it. I contemplate it.

My memory is very calendrical. If no such word as calendrical exists, I've probably invented it. It means guided, informed or pertaining to the calendar. In my mind's eye I see calendars floating everywhere...just kind of hovering in mid air. Sort of like icons on a computer desktop or apps on a smart phone. I click on whatever I want to enter. If somebody asks me about December 5, 1980, I immediately see a timeline in my head, floating up there in space with 1980 pushing its way up front in a Mandelbrot Set effect...the fractal being a calendar marked December, as the zoom lens of mid-air pulls up Friday the fifth so close that I'm transported back to that day. I'm suddenly *inside* it. I automatically know I'm in fifth grade, and I'm on the school playground playing kickball with my class. As I'm running from second base to third base, someone charges into me and knocks me well into the outfield where I land on a rock, splitting my head open. I remember this Friday not only because of such a traumatic event, but because John Lennon was still alive, and come Monday, he'd be dead.

At the age of ten, I wasn't yet a Beatles fan and wasn't all that familiar with Lennon or his music. I'd heard of the Beatles, but for reasons beyond my comprehension I thought they were Elton John's backing band. Honestly the reason for that was because the four-year old me in 1974 once asked one of the neighbors what her favorite band was. She said "Elton John and the Beatles. All I ever listen to is Elton John and the Beatles." So, not yet being hip to many bands and artists, I interpreted Elton John and the Beatles as one band. At that young age, the Beatles were obviously not that impressionable on me. Yet, it was the event of Lennon's murder six years later, and the way in which it haunted the news for weeks that left an indelible impression on me for the rest of my life. I remember some teachers crying the morning after it was announced. My teacher kept mentioning it all week and saying how sad she was and how important Lennon was to her and to the rest of the world. At this point in life, I was still listening to my Kiss records and was just beginning to branch out in my interest in rock music. I really had no idea. From the way the adults were acting though, I knew something big and horrible had happened.

Seven years passed from 1980 before I began to feel personally effected by the death of Lennon. On December 8, 1987, I was hanging out in the bedroom with WNEW-FM on in the background as it always was. They played one of those "today in music" segments where they recounted 1980's WNEW Christmas concert, an annual fundraiser that featured a different artist each year. The narrating voice of this short segment spoke about the event of that year (a concert by the Marshall Tucker Band) as a success, and briefly mentioned how everyone was feeling festive and in good spirits, and how the good cheer of the holiday season was present throughout the evening. And then in words spoken in a changing tone that I'll never forget...

"It was an evening that went from the highest high...to the lowest low."

Suddenly the narrator's voiceover cuts to a clip from the night of December 8, 1980. The voice is Vin Scelsa's. He doesn't sound his usual talkative self. In fact, his voice is trembling and hesitant. He then says something to the effect of..."I just got an official report that John Lennon died tonight." Then an uncomfortable silence rarely heard on live radio. Scelsa continues.

"I...I...I'm at a loss for words. I think for the first time in my career on radio I don't have anything to say."

There in my bedroom, following those words, I was instantly hit with a flashback of my initial experience with Lennon's murder. I remembered not fully knowing about him or how significant his death was. I also remembered the ill feeling of knowing something extra terrible had happened by the way so many adults were crying. It was a memory that I suppose I'd hidden since then, or blocked out so to speak. By this point in my life, at 17, I had a much better perspective on the history of rock music, and through this brief radio clip, was hearing for the first time what it sounded like if you had learned of Lennon's death from radio that night. Let's remember...there was no Internet. You couldn't just pull up these clips on Youtube. This was a recording of Scelsa as he spoke on that very night of Lennon's murder, and it probably hadn't been heard in the seven years since. Needless to say, the sound of a broken-up Scelsa left a heavy impression on me, almost as scarring as the event itself through the eyes of an unknowing child.

From that moment, December 8, 1980 was never at any time all that far from my imagination. For the better part of my adult life, John Lennon's murder has been something of an obsession. It's followed me around. I've studied, dissected and analyzed the shit out of the subject from every angle possible. I even wrote a book about it! I can't begin to count how many times I've stood outside the Dakota trying to envision his view every time he left home and walked out on the street, so freely and unprotected. Of all the celebrities and music artists who can't go anywhere without bodyguards, Lennon was one of the four most famous people in the world. We don't have to go over the importance of the Beatles. In the world of music, there was the Beatles and there was everyone else.

Period.

But there were only four of them.

Four people who wrote and recorded a major chunk of the greatest music of our lifetime. And one of them trusted mankind so much, that he put himself out there unprotected and accessible to anybody who wanted to meet and talk with him.

You wanted to meet Paul McCartney? Good luck, it just wasn't going to happen. Want to meet Mick Jagger? Yeah, right.

But if you wanted to meet John Lennon, you knew to stand outside the Dakota for a while and eventually he'd come out...or you could catch him while he was walking in. And even back then, long before the word *stalking* became an everyday vocabulary word in the tabloid press and the pop culture it reflected, you couldn't just stand around and meet a celebrity. It didn't work that way, even back then. Most stars were inaccessible, and the thought of even getting near someone was far-fetched. Not with Lennon.

And so he went out one night in early December unprotected just as he always did, and he came home to meet the bullets that ended his life. Almost eight years later in October 1988, I went with a bunch of friends to the opening night of *Imagine John Lennon*, the first and only real feature film with a theatrical release to celebrate the life and mourn the loss of Lennon. It had been almost a year since I heard the Scelsa flashback on the radio, and memories of that entire weekend in December 1980 began haunting me. I've heard of people blocking things out of their memory, but as someone who remembers everything, and more than most people, I've realized that I must have been blocking out Lennon's death as first experienced from the viewpoint of a ten-year old. And starting late in 1987, I began to remember it and think about it regularly. Within the course of the next year, I'd begin getting into the Beatles catalog very quickly. I went through a heavy metal phase during my teens, and at 18 I was outgrowing it with my tastes expanding and evolving. By the end of the summer of 1988, I'd been through every Beatles album and was around five albums into Bob Dylan's catalog. I'd taken a genuine interest in the counterculture of the 1960s and was beginning to let my musical tastes travel back 20-25 years. I'd just graduated high school, and as someone who hated school, got atrocious grades and found history boring, it was a remarkable transformation as I quickly began to delve into modern American history and pop culture as it was reflected through music. The Beatles, although from across the ocean, had left a permanent mark on the States, and the States had left a permanent mark on the Beatles. I identified mostly with John, and later on, George. Going into the fall of 1988, Lennon and Dylan's music had spoken to me in ways that no other music had ever done before. For the first time, lyrics began to take precedence over the music. It helped of course, that I liked the music of both artists, but for the first time in my life, I was getting things out of the words to songs that I never got in the metal stuff I'd been listening to for years. Bruce Springsteen was an exception through those metal years. But even though I knew I was finding something substantial in his music, my connection with the Boss was kept in the closet around my metalhead friends who were beyond redemption and caught up in the total superficiality of metal and the 1980s metal code, which read: *If you listen to any music other than metal, you're a fucking homo.*

Going into the theater in South Amboy, New Jersey on the night of Friday, October 7, 1988, I'd already been profoundly affected by Lennon's music in the months prior. *Imagine John Lennon* was set for release during the weekend of what would have been John's 48th birthday...so this was something we'd been looking forward to. When I say "we," I mean my core group of friends (Tom, Eric and Chris) along with a host of others associated with our group. It was true, what they said about graduating high school. Once you leave, you never see any of those people again. For many years, that was true. The Internet and social media didn't exist yet, so I left my judgmental metalhead friends back at the high school where I felt they were better off, and never saw them again until social media decades later. A few of them evolved and shed the metal posturing of their teen years and I enjoy seeing them to this day. But, in my pre-Facebook life, it was mostly just me and my inner circle of people with whom I've always been unapologetically myself. There were at least a dozen of us in the theater. I remember some girls who were there to hang out with Chris were talking through most of it, and Tom got agitated and quietly got out of his seat toward the back of the theater and went to sit by himself down front. For some reason, that always sticks out when I think of that movie. Regarding the movie itself, I only ask you, the reader, to put in perspective the timeframe we're dealing with. It had only been eight years since we lost John Lennon. A lot of the footage we've seen so much of and often take for granted had not been seen before. At the young age of 18, I was still soaking everything in. Watching this film was an experience of one revelation after another. By the time it ended with the expected and inevitable death report and aftermath footage, I lost it. The credits rolled, the lights went on and people filed out of the room while I remained in my seat looking down and trying to hide the fact that I had tears flowing down my face. I took several minutes before I got up to go meet my friends out in the parking lot.

And so, on the night of July 8, 2010, sometime between 10:30 and 11:00, I drive away from the White Castle with my number one and an extra bacon cheddar slider. Being the obsessive that I am, there isn't a goddamn thing that I don't consider or think of going into any situation. I miss nothing. That means don't ever try to pull one over on me because it will backfire on you, even as it's happening. That said, it hits me as I drive home...John Lennon and I were born at different times of the day. If I were measuring my time on the planet against John's, I would have been dead a few hours already since I was born earlier in the day than John was. But the drama of the evening that John's murder took place is far too indelible not to recreate in my mind in real time. So I ignore the fact that I'm dead, and keep driving.

From this point forward, I will just refer to Lennon as John where applicable. I've spent enough hours of thought, discussion and interviews concerning John Lennon over the years and have already written one book about him and have therefore earned the use of first-name basis in how I refer to him. So, I pull up to the house that I share with two friends, and I park the car. As I glance out, I envision the police arriving at the Dakota in response to shots fired on Seventy-Second Street. I grab my Coke and White Castle bag, get out of the car, close the door and head up the walkway toward the stairs of the house. Jose Perdomo, the doorman at the Dakota is pointing out the guy who shot me. He has a copy of *Catcher in the Rye* with him. It's one of my very favorite books. Pretty soon, he's going to use it as his reason for killing me. He sees me as an innocent about to be corrupted. He sees himself as Holden Caulfield and he needs to free me by removing me from the planet, never once stopping to consider that Holden Caulfield, as confused and miserable as he was, never hurt anybody.

I go in the house and shut the door. My two friends, Stick and Stick are comatose on the couch. The television is on showing Woody Allen's *Interiors*. Both Sticks are looking at the television, but neither of them can see it. I sit down at the table in the kitchen and begin inhaling my food, barely chewing it. Just devouring it. I think of John Travolta in *Saturday Night Fever* as he's shoving the burgers into his fat Tony Minero face and his friends are ridiculing him for not chewing.

Big chunks of hamburger going down my throat.

Dog Friskies.

Dog yummies.

Ya know what, Joey? I'm gonna turn into a dog.

I sit staring into my food for longer than I would like to. After this is all over, it's around 11:10, and I head upstairs for a shower. As I'm lathering up my head with shampoo, my mind wanders over to Roosevelt Hospital where I'm in the hands of Dr. David Halleran. Throughout the rest of my shower, my mind is flashing on what the chaos in and around the emergency room must have been like. I've often wondered what went through John's mind in those initial moments after he was shot. As freely as he lived, venturing around town unprotected on a daily basis, he still carried around a sense of paranoia until the day he died. There was always that sense of *they*.

Them.

The FBI.

The government.

After fighting to remain in the United States, a certain level of fear resided within him. Richard Nixon had an FBI file taken out on him less than a decade before. Even though John was indeed concerned about being followed and killed, there has never been one single shred of worthy evidence that even remotely proves the conspiracies that the incoming Republicans had him killed. Still, once he was hit by those bullets, there had to have been something going through his mind, even if only for a fraction of an instant where he thought, "They finally did it. They got me."

He never got to know his killer the way we did. He was never told why he was killed, yet *we* were given very specific reasons for it. Yet, for a brief flashing second after hearing his name called, followed by the burst of gunfire that ripped four holes in his body with extreme precision, John must have thought or at least wondered what the hell kind of government order was behind it. Needless to say, this is only my own speculation. In the book I wrote on the murder, I barely acknowledge the conspiracy theories and will give no further attention to them here. Of course there also remain the conspiracy theories that suggest Jose the Doorman, a supposed former CIA agent, was the real shooter, but that's neither here nor there, and it doesn't really matter. Either way, John Lennon was still fucking dead.

I step out of the shower and dry myself off at around 11:20. It's at this moment that I'm pronounced dead. Years later, I have an epic phone call with the two main nurses who worked on John when he was killed, and they confirm for me that he was pronounced dead at 11:15, not 11:20 as most accounts suggest. I throw on some shorts and a t-shirt and head to the living room where my two friends are still seated in the same spots, their heads bobbling around in Oxycontin nods. I lay down on the other couch pinning the hair on the back of my head to the pillow. My hair has been in that shit stage between short and long that happens when you start to let it grow. It has a natural wave to it, so I lay against a pillow to make it dry straight. Summer is a bitch. The TV is still on but nobody is watching it. I fall into a deep zone-out trance reflecting on the past night. I have to think for a moment.

Wait.

What did I do tonight? What kind of night was it?

Then I remember that I'm dead.

Wait.

Why again am I dead?

Then I remember.

Oh yeah.

John Lennon.

At that moment, it hits me. I'm not dead at all. In fact, I'm very much alive. And after growing up under the shadow of the Beatles, this intimidating everlasting presence of rock and roll myth, legend and majesty, and idolizing people like John Lennon...I realize that I've now been on the planet longer than he was...and Jimi...and Brian... and Janis...and Otis...but in one profound and sobering revelation, I also realize that I will not by any means outlive any of them.

2

BAREFOOT IN SUBURBIA

Growing up as an early teen, it always seemed to me that the few cool kids that I actually liked had stereos and listened to vinyl records while all the assholes had boom boxes and played cassettes. These were most of the popular kids who always walked around with their boom boxes and often brought them to school. I do realize I'm generalizing here, but really...every asshole I knew just happened to carry a boom box around in public.

There was a social element to music. When kids got together, someone always had their boom box playing the latest AC/DC or Rush album on cassette. Cassettes were in full swing and everyone seemed to not mind them. I personally hated everything about them and actually resented their existence. The other kids didn't get it. They didn't see the imposter nature of a new physical format of music.

They didn't care about holding an album cover in their hand along with all the wonder, speculation and imagination that accompanied that experience. Liner notes, lyrics and gatefolds were not yet part of the cassette package. At this early stage of the technology, you were just given a slab of cardboard paper with a picture of the album cover folded into a hard plastic case that usually cracked. Cassettes were concise and compact and you could carry them around with your boom box while you were out with your friends hanging in the malls or on the streets. Kids who were into the trends and trying to be popular treated music as a social occasion, or more accurately something to serve as the *backdrop* to social occasions. Kids serious about the music didn't listen to it with groups of friends while hanging outside the Space Port arcade. They listened by themselves in their bedrooms. The music was to be focused upon. The music demanded attention. They played air guitar and air drums, taking in every note, every beat and every word, and it meant something. But not just something. It was everything. That pretentiousness was my attitude at the age of 13.

I wasn't sure what I was on to at that early age, but I knew I didn't like it. I saw cassettes as symbols of early 1980s trends that the popular kids followed. Their music collections reflected the changing times... simple as that. Cassettes, they said were going to replace vinyl. In reality, what they really replaced was the 8-track tape. Boom boxes subbed for stereos. It was perhaps the very first experience with change that anyone of my generation had stumbled upon, and right from the outset, I fucking hated it. Sure...like everyone else, I owned cassettes. Lots of them. My stereo had a cassette player and so did my first three cars. That said, it was the first time we noticed a shift in what we thought was normal and eternal. Not every change however was reflected in technology. Most were reflected in the constant evolution of music over the next four decades, and in the different branches and offshoots of styles and genres that would inevitably plague the very dignity of musical vitality. How many times over the years going straight back to the 1970s would they say "rock is dead" before it actually died the pathetic whimpering death that it eventually did? How many times?

But that's for later discussion.

Metal.

Metal was a pre-requisite to popularity. It didn't guarantee it, but it was one of the requirements to fitting in with certain packs of kids. Once middle school happened, it was becoming awfully hard to exist on The Who and The Stones alone. Everyone I knew seemed to be gravitating toward metal. I remember turning on MTV and seeing the video for Iron Maiden's "Run to the Hills," and being completely repulsed by the galloping beat and the melody of the chorus...Bruce Dickinson wailing *"Ruuunnn toooo thaaaaa hiiiiiiilllls! Ruuuunnn fo-ooorrr yourrr li-iii-iiiiiffffffe!"*

I thought about seventh grade, and how much I hated it. I thought about all the kids I hadn't known prior to seventh grade, and how they just suddenly appeared in seventh grade, and how I only associated them with seventh grade. I carried that hideous chorus melody around with me for days. Weeks. That fifteen seconds of Maiden left an imprint in my brain that I couldn't get rid of. There was also a kid I didn't like. He was one of the school bullies and I was often his target in gym class when I sucked at volleyball. He was always wearing an Iron Maiden *Number of the Beast* shirt. To this day, *Number of the Beast* remains my least favorite Maiden album of the 1980s, and it's definitely by far the most overrated. But that's not because of the asshole kid, but because I just never cared for it as an album, not to mention the fact that I got sick and tired of Maiden fans telling me it's their best album. But at some point, I'd come to a realization that our dislike of people often contributes to our dislike of the music we associate with them. It wasn't all that different from our dislike of sports teams. It explained my childhood hatred of the Miami Dolphins. One of the neighborhood bullies was a Dolphins fan. But it was during the summer after that seventh grade school year where I felt compelled to get into this music by all means and at all costs. So I went out and bought Iron Maiden's latest album, *Piece of Mind*.

Oh yeah, a little side note...I had already been listening to Judas Priest by this time, via some cassette tapes I recorded off of my best friend, Tom's albums. See? Cassettes!

Judas Priest, I liked instantly. They weren't like Maiden who only had four albums out. There was something nice about having an entire catalog of a dozen albums or so ahead of me. It was like being six years old and discovering Kiss for the first time, and having all those album covers in front of me while visiting *Two Guys* record department. ..all those album covers that gnawed at my curiosity. What did those records sound like? This is what happened with Judas Priest. I knew all of the album titles and song titles before I even heard them. It captured my imagination enough to the point where I was writing down the names of every Priest song in my school notebooks...but not just writing them down, but grouping them with their corresponding albums, and writing them down in the exact running order. I became obsessed, and eventually my school work suffered. This was around the beginning of eighth grade which happened in the fall of 1983. While this was going on, Quiet Riot's *Metal Health* grabbed America by the testicles and reached the top of the almighty Billboard charts. It was the first time a metal album hit the number one spot. Something was clearly happening, and the middle schools and high schools in New Jersey's Middlesex County seemed to be just a microcosm of what was going on throughout America. Metal had arrived on the mainstream. Revisionist history over the past decade assigns 1980 as the big breakout year in metal, and that may very well be true in the U.K. It's why critics always abuse the most overused phrase of metal fans...*New Wave of British Heavy Metal.* What happened overseas in 1980 wasn't the case in the States. Perhaps this take can be viewed as America-centric, but not really. As an American, this is the only firsthand perspective I can give. Plus, it's not an opinion...it's the way it happened. In the States, 1983 marked the golden age of metal and is by far more of a breakout year for metal than 1980 ever was. 1980 unquestionably had some great album releases...nothing more, nothing less. 1980 didn't have MTV. 1983 saw metal bands not only infiltrating the pop charts, but because of MTV, it was 100 percent more visually available to mainstream audiences, as key influential acts like Priest and Maiden who both spent 1980 in opening act slots were now headlining 20,000-seat arenas around the world. If there is one standout event to mark the golden age of metal in the States, it is no question, Day 2 of the second US Festival, held in San Bernardino, California on May 29, 1983. That was the day metal put the rest of the world on notice.

That October, my neighbor asked me if I wanted to go see Iron Maiden at the Garden with him. He was a year older than me and had a lot more freedom than I'd ever dreamed of. My first thought was *holy shit...Iron Maiden! At Madison Square Garden!* I'd never been to the Garden before. That place held 20,000 people! Were they really that big? Hadn't they just opened for Judas Priest a year before? My next thought was *no way am I gonna be allowed to go to that.* And I wasn't. A few weeks later, my same neighbor told me he was going to see Black Sabbath and Quiet Riot at the Meadowlands. Something was indeed happening.

Up to the age of 13, I'd been to lots and lots of concerts in my life, but they were all Frankie Valli and the Four Seasons concerts. My parents were big fans and it was literally the very first music I was exposed to. My first show was at Convention Hall in Asbury Park during the summer of 1974. We had third row seats and at the end of the show, my dad held me up over the front of the stage so Frankie Valli could shake my hand. Other shows however, were an impossibility during early childhood. Late in 1977, Kiss played three nights at the Garden on their *Alive II* tour, or as some still call, the *Love Gun* tour...all the same thing if you ask me. I begged my mom to get me tickets. She called Bambergers where she happened to work at the Ticketron and inquired about tickets. Then she shook her head while still holding the phone. No tickets available. All sold out. I personally think it was a fake phone call with nobody on the other end, as was the call she made two years later for the *Dynasty* tour. Again, she did the same thing for Bruce Springsteen's *River* shows at the Garden near the end of 1980. Truth be told, those concerts were sold out and tickets weren't even a possibility for most people. Looking back, I've often wondered why my dad hadn't tried to get us Springsteen tickets in 1980 considering he had the *Darkness on the Edge of Town* and *River* albums, and liked both of them. I suppose it wasn't anything that he cared deeply enough to pursue.

Tom and I took a little more of a pro-active approach when we heard Judas Priest would be coming to the Meadowlands in support of their brand new *Defenders of the Faith* album. We were both pushing 14 and weren't as willing to just accept and believe that our parents had put in an honest effort to secure tickets. My mom no longer worked at the Ticketron, but Tom's mom had a connection through which we were able to get three twelfth-row floor seats. Our parents were still overprotective and suspicious of these kinds of events and the types of riffraff they attracted, so unlike all of our friends who were going to the show in large groups, Tom and I were accompanied by my dad. Weeks before the concert, my parents reminded me over and over again of all the drugs at concerts and how I was going to the worst possible place on earth. But I didn't do drugs. And my dad was going to be there with us. What did they think was going to happen?

Looking back, I remember how terrified I was of the whole event. The idea that my dad was going to be at the concert with us was concerning to me, and I kept hoping that we wouldn't run into any of my friends who surely would be smoking and drinking and having the time of their teenage lives. There was also the fact that I was a shy timid kid around my family and was afraid of opening up and enjoying the music and the whole experience. Up to that point, the adults in our lives led us to believe that music was one giant interruption of life, and that I needed to "come down to reality." I suppose if Kiss and Judas Priest hadn't made me get so many bad grades, things would have been a little different? I often wonder if I had been a good student in school and gotten good grades, if my parents would have given Kiss and Judas Priest some credit the same way they gave them the blame.

When we got to the show on that night of March 23, 1984, we were led down to our seats by an usher. The Meadowlands Arena, then named after a former governor named Brendan Byrne, was still fairly new at the time. I had been there a whole bunch of times for Nets and Devils games (I was a fan of neither, but my uncle used to score crazy amounts of tickets and was always giving them to us), and was always sitting either up in section 213 for hockey or down in 105 on the lower level for basketball. This was the first time I was going to be down on the floor, and was awestruck as we walked the length of the aisle toward the stage. It wasn't the stage that had my attention though... it was the view from the floor looking up at the two tiers of seats that wrapped around the arena. I finally had a view of what it looked like from a basketball and hockey player's perspective. I thought that was pretty cool. As we sat there waiting for the lights to go down, I kept looking all around me, trying to soak in what the place looked like from the floor. I think at the time, I had an arena/stadium fixation and was always studying the architectural layouts of places like the Meadowlands, Shea Stadium, Yankee Stadium, Madison Square Garden, etc..

When the lights went down, the venue was still half empty, and it dawned on us that we had no idea who the opening act was going to be. By the time the opening act's set was over, we still had no idea who the opening act was, although they were called Great White and were so new that they didn't even have an album out yet. Tom later found their EP a few months after the show. I remember them playing "Substitute" by the Who, which seemed to be lost on the metal crowd. By the time the intermission was over and the lights went down for Priest, the place erupted in thunderous chaos. M-80s rocked the building and green fluorescent light sticks were hurled through the air recklessly and nonstop. As the band slammed into the opening chords of "Love Bites," the sight of the giant Metallian were first visible to the crowd. The horned half monster, half tank featured on the cover of *Defenders of the Faith* became the enormous backdrop to a stage set lined with two floors of wall-to-wall Marshall stacks. The Defenders tour became one of Priest's most visually undocumented tours and no real footage from it existed publically until something surfaced around 2006. To this day, there is only one bootlegged video of a complete *Defenders* concert, which happens to be from the Montreal Forum, which took place just three nights before our show. Carrying the visuals of that night for the next twenty-something years with nothing more than memories of it in my head...my first true rock concert experience, it became something of a Holy Grail moment when I finally saw moving footage of the show on Youtube. It brought me right back to that Friday night. Earlier in the day I came home from school, went to my guitar lesson, and my dad picked me up. From there, we picked up Tom and headed for the Meadowlands. The next morning, we'd have to be in church by eight for confirmation rehearsal. But that didn't matter. That night, I screamed and I screamed loud. Something just took over me and suddenly it became a matter of making my voice heard, as if Rob Halford and the Priest themselves were going to *hear* my voice and distinguish it from the rest of the crowd, as if it mattered. As if one kid not screaming along would have made much difference in a sea of 17,000 people. To me, it did make a difference, and I couldn't just sit back and simply observe the party. I had to be part of it. I shouted back the lyrics as Priest played song after song. I didn't care how crazy I looked to my dad if he happened to glance over at me at any time during the show. This was my first true experience in being totally one with the music, where nothing could penetrate my state of mind. I don't even think Tom and I communicated or even looked at each other during that show. Just two young teens rocking out in their own personal party with Judas Priest, where tens of thousands of other people just happened to be. Every once in a while, I'd glance over at my dad who was standing on his seat next to Tom. He looked horrified. He seemed to be taking in the entire experience from his own adult perspective, not necessarily watching the show, but watching the entire room and the people in it. To go from sitting in a seat in a quiet venue while watching Frankie Valli with a civilized audience, and politely clapping after each song...to *standing* on a seat in the middle of thousands of wasted, screaming maniacs while the band played ear-splitting noise and blockbuster explosions rocked the building structure must have been a dreadfully painful experience in a frightening and barbaric environment. When the show ended, the lights went on and the inside of the arena was one giant hazy cloud of pot smoke. The three of us stepped off our seats and began walking toward the center aisle. My dad led the way. As we got to the end of our row, he turned around to look and me and Tom. He smiled and shook his head.

"You guys gotta be kiddin' me."

That's rock and roll.

3

SEEDS

Three months before the Judas Priest concert, I went into school on Friday, December 9, 1983, and our English teacher, Mr. C was telling us about a benefit concert he attended the night before at the Garden. Mr. C was really the only cool teacher I ever had, and probably the only teacher in all my middle and high school years who ever taught me anything important. He was a walking rock and roll encyclopedia who had long shoulder-length hair, always wore black jeans and a black vest, and taught rock and roll classes as an after-school activity. The man was a legend in my hometown, and much of what I learned about the finer things in rock music and later on all of the arts came directly from him. That day, he spoke about the Ronnie Lane Appeal to ARMS Concert. Ronnie Lane was a member of the Small Faces and then the Faces, a band almost ten years broken up. Lane was very sick with Multiple Sclerosis, and his closest friends who happened to be 1960s and 1970s rock royalty teamed up for a series of charity shows that came to the call of Action into Research for Multiple Sclerosis. The show centered around the three big ex-Yardbirds guitarists, Eric Clapton, Jimmy Page and Jeff Beck. Other notables such as Charlie

Watts, Joe Cocker, Paul Rogers and Andy Fairweather Low performed as well. Aside from the reason everyone was there, the night became most known for Page's performance. Mr. C spoke to the class about the Led Zeppelin guitarist, who was just re-emerging after literally not touching a guitar for the three years following the death of drummer John Bonham. Page had spiraled into depression and further drug abuse and was finally resurfacing to help an old friend and play for some old fans. We hung on every word as Mr. C recounted Page playing a somber instrumental version of "Stairway to Heaven," a 12-year old song that had become by far the most popular rock song of our lives and of our generation. He told us, "Jimmy walked up to the microphone, and said *This next song isn't my song. This is our song.*" As an impressionable kid, hearing the teacher say that to us awakened my first experience with any sort of sentimentality toward music. Today "Stairway" is over half a century old. It's crazy to think it was only 12-years old back then and still so new...and yet was already so legendary and seemed so old.

If there was one lasting reverberation of the ARMS concerts that rang out until I got it out of my system, it was Jeff Beck. I was pretty well-versed in rock music by the time of middle school. I knew my shit. Beck, however, was somebody I'd only heard about. I knew exactly who he was, and had even seen his albums in the stores. I'd never heard his music though, and couldn't even imagine what it sounded like. So, fast-forward seven months to July 1984. I was in Shop Rite with my mom who was doing the weekly food shopping. My ritual for years would be to tag along and disappear into the magazine aisles or record department. Yes, even Shop Rite had a pretty decent collection of music at one time. I'd alternate music and magazines from week to week. Growing up in a pre-Internet world left us cut off from instant information. Perhaps "cut off" is not an accurate description because we never had instant information, leaving no chance of being cut off from something that didn't yet exist. We had 13 channels on TV, and only seven of them worked. Most of them had news, but only at certain times of the day. If we wanted to learn about stuff, we went to the library and took out a book on it. And if we wanted to find out music news or what was going on with our favorite bands, we waited for the new *Creem*, *Circus*, *Hit Parader* or *Rolling Stone* magazines to hit the stands. I'd run straight for the magazine section of Shop Rite once a week, and check each issue for news about new albums and tours. During the weeks of no new releases, I'd go to the record department and dream of having certain things in my collection. One day that summer, I found myself hovering over the Nice Price bin. The Nice Price bin was made up of cassettes of older albums from Columbia/CBS artists at a reduced cost. In that bin I found a copy of Jeff Beck's *Blow By Blow* for three dollars. I had some money in my pocket from mowing the lawn, so I decided to buy it. Returning home to listen to it, I had no idea what to expect, but sure didn't think it would all be instrumental. I liked what I heard though. It was lead guitar-driven and there was a smooth, chill, beautiful, haunting, even funky element to it that I dug. Yet, it was still fierce and intense. It was a pleasant difference from all of the metal I had been listening to. There was something intelligent about it that metal lacked. The three big albums for me during the summer of 1984 were as eclectic a mix as it got. Judas Priest's *Stained Class*, Jeff Beck's *Blow By Blow* and Bruce Springsteen's *Born in the U.S.A.* This doesn't mean these albums all came out in 1984, but that's what I was listening to. I'd been a Springsteen fan since the age of eight, but only recently went into the closet around my metal-head friends. There seemed to be a backlash against the Boss as he got more and more world famous due to the success of *Born in the U.S.A.* And Bruce wasn't a headbanger. He was just a regular rock and roll guy, which meant he wasn't cool by any metal standards. So I kept my love of his music to myself.

That summer, I also picked up the July 1984 edition of *Guitar World,* which featured Glenn Tipton and KK Downing of Judas Priest on the cover. I spent a few months with that issue, literally reading every article, which is not something I've done very often with magazines. Besides the cover story, there was an article about Michael Sembello, the singer of the 1983 hit, "Maniac," as well as a really great piece on Nile Rodgers. It was a story on a relatively unknown guitarist from Sweden named Yngwie Malmsteen though, that got enough of my attention to keep returning to it, reading it over and over again. Yngwie was 20 years old and had only been living in America for a year and a half. Upon arriving on the West Coast on February 6, 1983, he joined a new metal band called Steeler, led by vocalist Ron Keel. Word-of-mouth quickly spread of this guitarist's unique sense of speed and shred unlike anything ever heard before, and Steeler was playing to packed clubs until Graham Bonnet called. The former Rainbow and Michael Schenker Group vocalist was putting together a new band and needed a guitarist worthy of his ego. Coming off projects with Schenker and Ritchie Blackmore, Bonnet wanted somebody exceptional and had heard about Yngwie who jumped at the chance. Alcatrazz was quickly formed, releasing their first album *No Parole From Rock and Roll* late in 1983. There had been nothing of Alcatrazz on my radar through much of 1984, at least not in the States. But in reading the article, I recognized the name and recalled hearing "Island in the Sun" on the radio while driving out to Shea Stadium with my dad to see the very last Jets football game in December 1983. They were introduced by the DJ (presumably WNEW or WAPP at the time) as a brand new band. Long story short, what was to be a new band serving as a vehicle to feature Bonnet as the star, quickly became all about Yngwie Malmsteen stealing the show and becoming the center of attention with both fans and critics. Long story short, by the end of summer, a brand new independent record store called Vintage Vinyl appeared right around the block from where I lived. It was in the same stripmall as the A&P where we often got milk, and the old Drug Fair that became a Rite Aid. And the old arcade we used to play video games in. And Angelo's pizza where many a birthday party was held. I point all this out to emphasize how fucking badass it was to have an independent record store walking distance from my house. Walking in for the first time, I was blown away. This was no average *Sam Goody*, *Record Town*, or *Music Den*. You weren't going to find Sheena Easton or Barbara Mandrell in there. You were more likely to find Kate Bush and Alcatrazz. They specialized in metal, hardcore punk, and what would later become known as alternative. Still, you could find all the classic stuff like Beatles and Stones sitting right across from the Crucifucks and Lizzy Borden. In the next aisle you could find Julian Cope. It was in Vintage Vinyl where I finally picked up a copy of the Alcatrazz album as well as Yngwie Malmsteen's first solo album, *Yngwie Malmsteen's Rising Force*. That was the start of the next phase of my teenage life.

I spent much of my years between 14 and 16 grounded for bad report cards, so spent lots and lots of time in my bedroom where I spent every hour away from school learning Yngwie Malmsteen solos by ear.

I could sweep arpeggios like a motherfucker and everyone knew it, yet my short hair wouldn't allow me into any bands, nor did any of the "cool kids" want to play with me. During this period, I started listening to a lot of instrumental guitarists. They became a dime a dozen, all following on the heels of Malmsteen's album. It seemed that all of my guitar player friends had a different guitarist to worship every month. One month it was Yngwie. The next month it was Tony MacAlpine. The month after that, it was Vinnie Moore. After a while, it became impossible to tell anybody apart from each other. In much the same way that it took a real man to distinguish between Picasso and Braque during their Cubist periods, it took a real man to distinguish between MacAlpine and Moore in 1986.

1986 was also the year that saw the three-way split of metal. This divide can be traced back to 84 and 85 however, and its gradual emergence unfolded over these two years. And yes, we can trace this all and contain it within this one chapter, so relax and consider the following...

At the outset, let's look at the first half of the decade. During the early Eighties, metal's existence was rather clear and definitive. And it was well understood who the two reigning powerhouses were. Judas Priest and Iron Maiden were it. Period. Everything else, while impressive and often quite good, was inferior. These two bands were the template by which every other band and formula was designed. No, that's not to suggest that they were the first bands to feature screaming vocalists surrounded on either side by twin axes shredding dual-harmony guitar solos, and silly cartoon drawings on their album covers. It just means that Priest and Maiden perfected it enough to set the standards for a while. Aside from musical structure, the visuals of a band were usually leather, studs, chains, spandex, ripped t-shirts and occasional denim. It was a tough image with a dash of flash here and there. Priest and Maiden among middle school and high school students were the two rival bands that fans would fight over. Who was the better band? What band had the better vocalist? What guitar duo was better? Who had better album covers? The Priest and Maiden rivalry was friendly though, quite akin to the Beatles/Stones rivalry between fans in the Sixties. There was a reason for that, and that's that it was almost impossible to not like both bands. Priest fans liked Maiden, and Maiden fans still liked Priest. Yet, there always remained the question. Were you a Priest person or a Maiden person? Prior to the divide, Priest and Maiden reigned over a metal world that grew increasingly popular, but increasingly more commercial. But what was that world made up of? Well, Ozzy Osbourne had left Black Sabbath for a solo career that blew up bigger in its first four years than Sabbath had ever been with or without him. Sabbath, completely dead in the water by the time Ronnie James Dio had come aboard was no longer the major entity it once was, nor would it ever be again. *Heaven and Hell* and *Mob Rules* were stylistic blueprints for what would become Dio's solo career much more than they were Sabbath albums that could sit alongside the classic albums with Ozzy without the anal retentive fan feeling the need for an asterisk. There is nothing worse as a fan than having to compartmentalize your band's history into eras according to how many times they switch singers or guitarists. So by the time Dio left the band, Sabbath was a non-entity. They would attempt many stunts like getting a Gillan or two here and there, but they were hardly a major player by 1984. That world also contained AC/DC who were three albums into the Brian Johnson era. *Back in Black* was instantly monolithic, and would weave itself into the eternal echo of colossal album sales. The follow-up, *For Those About To Rock, We Salute You* proved a worthy successor but didn't come near the numbers or accolades. Nothing would. In 1983, they'd release *Flick of the Switch* and it would pass unnoticed. It would be the first album of the rest of AC/DC's history, and although they would release some great songs from time to time over the next thirty years, *Flick of the Switch* would also be the first of the band making the same formulaic album over and over again. I liken AC/DC in 1983 to the Rolling Stones. It has been universally suggested and agreed upon that *Tattoo You* was the last Stones album that anybody really gave a crap about. In 1983, they released *Undercover* and from there on, a new Stones album became just an excuse for a tour (though the Stones wouldn't tour on that particular go-round). *Flick of the Switch* was AC/DC's *Undercover*. While the giants of the previous decade were either floundering or doing well as solo acts, some newer blood was flowing in the form of Def Leppard, Quiet Riot, Motley Crue and Ratt. All would have moderate to major success on both MTV as well as FM radio by 1984. There were also a couple of 1970s acts that inevitably got thrown in with this scene. New York City's already-legendary Twisted Sister was scoring massive success by the summer and fall of 1984, and Van Halen, by far the biggest of the West Coast bands had grown to enormous popularity steadily on a year-by-year basis. By 1984, they were at their peak and still in their prime.

But were Van Halen really metal?

What about a new band called Bon Jovi? They were playing catchy keyboard-dominated rock, had long teased-up hair, cliché song structures and a pretty boy lead singer that dressed in denim and spandex, but bared no musical resemblance to metal. Yet all of these bands fell under the blanket of metal...somehow all ending up in magazines like *Circus* and *Hit Parader* while systematically ignored by *Rolling Stone.* While Van Halen may have been the early prototype for what would later become known as the hair band, Motley Crue was doing more for informing what hair bands would look like. In 1985, they released their third album, *Theater of Pain*, and the image that went along with it made them look more like women on the losing end of a fight with a can of hairspray as opposed to the street-tough Kiss wannabes they originally started out as. Over the course of the summer of 85, certain bands were putting the finishing touches on their respective new albums, and all would emerge looking much different from their 1984 incarnations. Ratt added lace and sequins to their leather and looked a lot more glamorous for their *Invasion of Your Privacy* album than they did a year before for their *Out of the Cellar* outing. Kiss crawled out of Bea Arthur's closet looking far more ridiculous than anyone upon the release of *Asylum,* wearing bad perms with pink, yellow and green fluorescent trench coats and leotards. The unmasked Kiss in 1985 wore more makeup than when they actually wore makeup. Within a year, we'd see the arrival of Cinderella and Poison and a whole lot of hot pink color schemes. By mid-1986 most acts associated with metal looked more like women than men, and the ones that still looked like men to a certain degree just added lots of color to their wardrobe. The color scheme of *Theater of Pain* is where this trend begins. Hair on the other hand became bigger for all involved. Even Priest and Maiden added some color to their look along with teased hair, although Maiden never really followed the hair trend. And Ozzy? Forget it. The Prince of Fucking Darkness re-emerged in 1986 as a frosted blonde wearing a sequin robe. The final ingredient for the major players such as Ozzy, Priest and Maiden in commercializing their sound was the guitar synth, which was present on their respective albums, *The Ultimate Sin*, *Turbo* and *Somewhere in Time*.

Something else was happening as 1984 turned to 85. The surge in thrash, power metal, death metal, black metal or whatever-the-fuck-else metal that had been quietly breaking out in little pockets around America had reached the suburbs and found its way into the high schools. Upon entering my freshman year, I found the cool kids and they took a liking to me. I looked a little on the geeky side and didn't do any of the risky things they did, but there was enough word-of-mouth that I was a badass guitar player that they took me under their wing. It was funny. Nobody would take me seriously enough to be in their band because I didn't have long hair, but the popular burnouts and musicians strangely respected me as a guitarist and took me in as a sort of mascot all through high school. Let this be an example of just how superficial metal was. You had to have long hair. Period. So what exactly was happening? By the time I fell in with the cool kids, there was one in particular who seemed to have a handle on all of the bands that most kids didn't know about. He was on the cutting edge of everything, and when he asked me what I liked and I proudly said Priest, his response took me by surprise. He told me yeah Priest was cool, but they weren't where it was at. Priest was old news. They weren't the future. He told me the future was a new band called Metallica, and he told me they were the fastest and heaviest band in the world. Their albums were hard to find, but I could get them in Vintage Vinyl. Within a few months, the Metallica buzz spread throughout the school and I imagine schools all over the country...because by the end of that year, Metallica had signed a major deal with EMI. During the course of that school year, kids were always coming up to you with a different album or cassette telling you "hey listen to this...this band is faster than Metallica! This band is heavier than Metallica!" Suddenly, the kids were listening to bands like Slayer, Venom, Exciter, Manowar, Metal Church, Overkill, Merciful Fate, and all kinds of scary shit. I liked Metallica for a while, and a few Manowar albums, but I kept a respectful distance from all the other stuff. Just too fast and abrasive for my personal taste. Plus, I was still trying to master harmonic minor scales while following Yngwie Malmsteen's early career. And so, by 1986, the three-way divide in metal had become clearly defined...the mainstream core of metal that had previously existed, the glam metal, aka hair bands...and thrash. Metalheads then became territorial and just plain fucking ridiculous.

Instantaneously, it became a matter of what band played heavier, whose drummer played faster, who was more satanic than whom, and who was more metal than whom. It became a war over what constituted "real metal." Metalheads became what the so-called punks in the 90s became, adhering to a self-imposed definition of what they wanted their genre to be. Certain metalheads, that is. The pre-requisite for "real metal" was Satan, or at the very least some evil scary theme. Now this is stuff Ozzy, Priest and Maiden had been doing for years. It had now become mandatory once Priest and Maiden started getting soft in their material, singing about being out in the cold, begging to be rescued, and lamenting over the golden years. I once read in some Maiden interview when *Somewhere In Time* was released, that "Wasted Years" was originally called "Golden Years," but they had second thoughts, not because it was already the title of a Bowie song, but because they didn't want anyone to make fun of them with a non-metal title such as that. I'm paraphrasing and don't quite remember who it's attributed to, but whoever in Maiden it was, said the original title sounded more like a wedding invitation than a metal song. The other essential for the uniform in which thrash fans had imposed on metal was speed. Then there was that band called Manowar that preceded the thrash movement, and they had already been using phrases like "false metal," even though they weren't all that much heavier than the bands who *played* false metal. Once Slayer took hold of the metalhead mentality, even finger-pointing bands like Manowar were no longer sufficient. And if you still listened to Priest and Maiden in 1987, you too were considered a poser. The Slayer fans were even pissing on Ozzy. Nothing was "real metal" to them unless it was a certain speed. Slayer fans greeted each other in class and out in the halls mouthing the "Raining Blood" riff, banging on the desks and lockers. They'd walk around all day screaming "SLAYAH!" It was their battle cry and it made them feel big and bad.

Non-metal acts like R.E.M., Bruce Springsteen, Bob Dylan, Prince, Barry Manilow and U2 didn't need battle cries.

Metal was different.

Metal needed to announce itself.

Point its finger.

Raise its fist.

But it wasn't quite the freak flag that Jimi Hendrix spoke of. The freaks weren't listening to metal. The freaks were listening to the Cure, Siouxsie and the Banshees, Sonic Youth, R.E.M,... The freaks were hippies...punks...goths...college intellectuals. They had asymmetrical haircuts and either wore tie dyes or blazers depending on if they were the intellectual type or just plain hippies. And they were into bands like the Cult long before the Cult began trying to appeal to metalheads who discovered them at *Sonic Temple*. But that's neither here nor there. The freaks and intellectuals became the future progressives and liberals...opting not to allow themselves to become bitter, angry adults who resented the fact that the white Christian male-dominated world around them wasn't quite etched in stone. They saw the value in the 1960s counterculture while metalheads tended to grow conservative as adults. Many embraced the Republican Party, while the ones who were too embarrassed to identify as Republicans, called themselves Libertarians. As kids, lots of metalheads weren't all that into social and political issues during the Eighties and consequently tend to identify in their adult life with the Eighties as something positive. They can't or don't in hindsight look too deeply into the consequences of the Reagan Eighties and merely identify the decade with their teen years. The party years. Shopping malls. Getting their driver's license. Getting laid. They identify with Ronald Reagan as their president, and they identify him as someone who was strong, powerful and good for the country. The reason I bring this up is to illustrate that metalheads weren't nearly as rebellious as they thought they were, nor were they the outlaws they pretended to be. They wanted more than anything to be accepted and fit into the mold they railed against.

But not all of metal had its head up its ass. Not the entire genre remained ignorant of the times. By 1987, while Steve Harris was still tastefully dipping into World History textbooks for inspiration, Rob Halford was still obsessed with iron claws and beasts dressed in black, and Ronnie James Dio was still writing about dragons and monsters that flew out of the sky, ripped your testicles off and force-fed them to you, Queensryche were writing their third full-length album, and they weren't about to reflect the one-dimensional world expected of most metal bands...demons, Satan and/or partying. But is that what Queensryche was? Were they really a metal band? Metal had splintered into so many different versions of itself and many were pointing more to prog. The term "progressive metal" came about later on with bands like Dream Theater, and other acts that could trace their sound back to a long lineage...which Queensryche sat right in the middle of. I remember a friend who looked down on metal referring sarcastically to Queensryche as "the thinking man's metal band."

By the early part of 1988, I was beginning to grow tired of the superficiality of metal as well as the overall sound of it. I started seeing it as something fake and ridiculous...cartoonish. I saw everybody who liked it as sheep who all looked the same, dressed the same, said the same things and acted the same way. Even the artsy-fartsy kids who listened to Depeche Mode started appearing cooler to me than the metal heads. At that point in time, Tom and I were both going back to the middle school at the end of the school day to visit Mr. C who we sorely missed. We'd always remembered how cool he was, and how real he was, and how he could never steer you wrong when it came to music. Halfway through senior year, he gave me a cassette of two R.E.M. albums that he recorded off his own vinyl. The 90-minute TDK was made up of *Life's Rich Pageant* and *Document*, R.E.M.'s two latest albums which grew on me immediately, probably because I *wanted* to like it. But I genuinely *did* like it. It rocked in ways that metal couldn't rock. It sure as hell wasn't nearly as heavy or fast in the "heavy" and "fast" parameters of metal...but it contained an element of hip that metal could never attain nor comprehend. How refreshing it was to listen to rock music that didn't contain lyrics about death and destruction and how fast you could go and how hard you could hit or how black it could get. There were poetic, political and ecological elements to this music. In short, it was intelligent…and it was where I needed to go.

When I first heard Queensryche's *Operation:Mindcrime* in early May of that year, I 'd already absorbed four R.E.M. albums and had been reading the New York Times, sometimes bringing it to school. Eventually, one of my metalhead friends began calling me Mr. Intellectual. I still had an ear for metal, but it was very specific things I was looking for. *Operation:Mindcrime* knocked me on my ass. In my daily reading, I began to learn about the upcoming election and how President Reagan maybe wasn't the hero they made him out to be when we were in fifth grade and we were told that he rescued the American hostages from Iran just by becoming president. Coinciding with these realizations, I bought *Operation:Mindcrime* the day it came out. In the first ten minutes of it, I heard Geoff Tate speaking to me in what initially seemed cryptic, as much metal did. But then I began making connections as he told me about the "seven years of power," the "corporation claw," and how the rich controlled the government, the media and the law. The lyrics called to "eradicate the Fascists" in Washington. He was of course referring to the Reagan Administration and the seven Reagan years so far, and suddenly I felt validated in how I had been feeling. Of course, for the record, let me make clear that at no time did I believe these were Tate's personal beliefs and I knew he was writing from the viewpoint of his characters...but the sentiment still stood. Finally, a metal band that actually had something to say!

Upon high school graduation, I went to visit Mr. C again. As a graduation present, he gave me four things that would change my life... two books and two albums. He gave me copies of Herman Hesse's *Siddhartha* and Jack Kerouac's *On the Road*. He also handed me copies of Bob Dylan's *Bringing it all Back Home* and *Highway 61 Revisited*. That summer I read both books within a few weeks and then began pouring through the Dylan albums. As his lyrics began to expand my understanding of human nature and art and culture and philosophy and God and the devil and the whole fucking universe, I suddenly realized about halfway through summer what Mr. C meant with his last words to me as he handed me those albums. I shook his hand and said, "Thanks, man. All of this isn't necessary." To which he only smiled.

"Seeds, man. They're seeds."

4

THE REAL 1989

It's mid August in New York City and it stinks like it. The ten-year old 1979 Datsun B-210 dumps us off on the corner of Sixth Avenue and West Eighth Street. I step onto the southeast corner where a bunch of table vendors are selling books in front of a B. Dalton bookstore and some self-righteous anti-pornography woman is prancing around holding up homemade signs adorned with giant anti-pornographic messages written in red marker next to some very vivid pornographic photos. In reality, the only pornography anywhere in sight is being exhibited by this woman, as she displays her images to the northbound traffic along the Avenue of the Americas. Across the street is a place called Gray's Papaya, a takeout hotdog joint that sells fruit drinks as their beverages. *How ingenious*, I think...a takeout hotdog place. We don't have those in Jersey. In fact, no fast food operations ever really gave much time, thought or attention to the hotdog. I also think, *how weird*...the marriage of hotdogs and papaya juice. The smell of hotdogs was always part of the New York of my imagination drawn from memories of childhood trips to the city...those midtown nights wandering around aimlessly with my aunt or cousin who took me to a museum uptown and then wanted to walk around Times Square or something...that smell of hotdogs, rotting garbage, sewage and piss left indelible marks on the walls of my brain any time I thought of New York City...so it's like stepping into some warped version of home from the corner of my mind as I cross West Eighth Street to go check out Gray's Papaya. I'm with Eric, my next door neighbor. I'm 19, he's 17, and we're both exploring the city for the first time on our own. For us, the city means the Village. Sure, we've been to baseball games and museums and musicals, and climbed to the tops of the Empire State Building and World Trade Center, and been to the South Street Seaport and been all around Uptown, Midtown and Downtown all accompanied by adults...but it's the music we're listening to along with the counterculture and Beatnik history that leads to our fascination with the Village...and the Village is where we need to be. Hence the advent of our bridge and tunnel lives.

It was at the tail end of the summer of 1989 when we became suburban hippies. Not all was about love in the city though. It was the summer of *Do the Right Thing* and the climate showcased onscreen mirrored the racial tension in real life. The Koch 1980s were in their final months and just on the verge of the Dinkins era. David Dinkins would become New York City's first black mayor just a few months later, defeating the tough-talking notorious racist prosecutor known as Rudolph Giuliani whose arrogant smirk and swagger wreaked of corruption in a manner that seemed to ask...*Oh Yeah? And just what the fuck are you gonna do about it?* The city was in its final decade of that gloriously icky, romanticized version of itself where the Village was still filled with the 1960s counterculture, Times Square was still a dangerous place filled with porn, hookers and cops, and New York still felt like New York. In the white suburbs, the 1960s had come full circle, which meant that they were back in fashion, and the music was being revisited by those who had lived it, and discovered in depth by those who were too young or not around at the time. It takes approximately 20-25 years for popular music to come full circle. Ten years after its heyday, it sometimes becomes irrelevant to what is currently happening, and is very often considered passé. After around twenty years, the nostalgia factor kicks in enough to make it all cool again. I'll explore this idea more extensively a little further ahead in Chapter 10.

That trip in August of 1989 was the first time I really explored Greenwich Village...this place that I'd heard so much about through word-of-mouth and through legend. That day, Eric and I spent hours wandering up and down West Eighth Street on a four-fold mission. First, hit the many clothes and shoe stores in search of the wardrobe that would make us look hipper than the average suburbanite. Everything we took home was covered in paisleys, flowers, stripes and mandalas, along with some Beatle boots, beaded necklaces and bracelets to go with it all. I personally went for more of an intelligent and artistic look than a hippie look, opting for blazers over tie dyes. My personal style always looked toward Patti Smith. Whatever Patti was wearing usually informed what I was wearing through most of my adult life. Second, we finally got to see the unorthodox collections of record stores like It's Only Rock and Roll and Revolver. These places were loaded with rare and out-of-print albums as well as bootlegs we never imagined existed, and stuff you couldn't get in Sam Goody. Just off the point where Eighth meets MacDougal, we finally made it to Psychedelic Solution, a store dedicated to psychedelic artwork and videos. The most shocking thing we found that really let us know where we were, was the vast collection of head shops lining West Eighth Street. Stores were unapologetically filled with glass cases of pipes and bongs of all sizes with no attempts at hiding them. It really felt as if we had entered an alternate universe that we had long imagined could exist someplace else, but just not in our own reality. And there it was...all right in front of our eyes. New York City.

It was in some ways a crossroads, 1989 was...a musical reckoning of sorts that culminated the past 25 years and set the tone for the next 25. Whereas the decade had been a rather dry and uncreative period for some of the biggest acts to come out of the 1960s and early 1970s, it proved to be downright embarrassing for others. By *embarrassing* I mean the same people responsible for giving us "White Rabbit" were also responsible for unleashing the diabolical "We Built This City" just 19 years later. Yes, these were the same people who screamed "UP AGAINST THE WALL MOTHERFUCKER!" As for dry periods, I don't necessarily mean there was no work from these bands or artists. Just not their best work. Bob Dylan entered the 1980s in his Christian phase with still two more gospel albums to turn out. In retrospect, the Christian era turns out to be a brilliant and highly respected body of work, albeit much too short-lived, though at the time, he was crucified for it, no pun intended. He followed that period up with the Mark

Knopfler-produced *Infidels*, one in a handful of albums post-1966 good enough to provoke the critical response "Dylan is back." However, Dylan quickly fell into a run of disoriented studio albums and mediocre-at-best live releases (*Real Live, Empire Burlesque, Knocked Out Loaded, Dylan and the Dead, Down in the Groove*). The Rolling Stones entered the Eighties extremely successful, and with a run of hit songs off back-to-back albums, *Emotional Rescue* and *Tattoo You*. The latter saw a world tour immortalized in Hal Ashby's concert film, *Let's Spend the Night Together*. It was a version of the Stones 12 years removed from Altamont, and it served as a visual documentation of what happens when a band gets so big on their name and history alone. Where rock began in its blues-on-the-front-porch embryonic stages and made its way toward the seedy clubs and dive bars, to well-promoted early rock and roll shows in theaters, to the arenas and eventual science experiments known as festivals where the occasional clusterfuck situation could arise, it settled mostly for theaters and arenas once the 1970s allowed a clear definition of what rock concerts were and what they could be. The acts of moderate popularity did the theaters and amphitheaters, while the larger acts played hockey arenas. Football stadiums were the last option before festival territory would have an audience set up in a vast sea of grass in the middle of nowhere. But football stadiums were mostly reserved for special one-off package jams such as JFK Jam, Texas Jam or Oakland's Day on the Green...events that saw anywhere from six to a dozen acts on the same bill. It wasn't often that one band would headline a stadium tour with only one smaller opening act. But that's exactly what a small handful of acts were able to do by the late Seventies and early Eighties. The Rolling Stones pretty much set the precedence for this...one of several in the rock world. I personally discovered the Stones in 1973 at the age of three when the second LP of their *Hot Rocks* album became a steering wheel in the imaginary car I drove. It was my uncle's album but I somehow inherited it when I went over his house and fucked it all up. My uncle was always messing with me when I was that young. He knew "The Immigrant Song" by Led Zeppelin scared the shit out of me, so he always made it a point to play it on the long four-legged console stereo that opened like a coffin. I'd hear that tiny hiss at the very beginning...that unmistakable sound right before the song starts...and it would immediately send me running into the next room where I'd dive behind the door to crouch into a fetal position and cover my ears before the inevitable wailing of Robert Plant's voice cried out that horrendous opening shriek that left me mortified. But as for the Stones, I was well aware of them by the age of three and I'd come to know many of their hits by the age of ten. Going into the 1980s, the Stones were pushing their late thirties and had long been thought of as *old*. I was in sixth grade during the 1981-82 school year when the *Tattoo You* tour happened, and word was out that it might be their last. This was never officially confirmed nor denied, but the Stones didn't tour again for another seven years. In between, they'd release two albums three years apart. Mick Jagger would fall prey to the worse trends of the decade and release a couple of embarrassing solo albums, as he and Keith Richards would feud. We'd hear about it in the news. Over a period of years, it became common accepted knowledge that the Stones were a thing of the past and it was never going to happen again. At least that was the consensus among rock fans as my teenage years progressed.

The guys in the Who were also pushing their late thirties as the decade began. Pete Townshend, Roger Daltrey, John Entwistle and

Kenny Jones decided to call it quits in 1982 and announced their Farewell Tour late in the summer. Jones, formerly of the Faces, had been the drummer for three years since the death of Keith Moon, and it radically altered the chemistry and dynamic of the band. Daltrey wasn't happy and Townshend still crawling through the abyss of drug and alcohol abuse had had enough of the rock and roll life and wanted to do other things. But whereas the Stones seemed to embrace the stadium circuit, it only made Townshend more contemptuous of the whole thing. On October 12, he'd sit in a limo on the way to Shea Stadium where the band was headlining the first of two nights, and instead of being appreciative of the opportunity to play to so many adoring fans, he'd express his disgust over how ridiculously huge and out of control rock had become. The takeaway from Townshend's miserable tone was something like... *What happens when the demand gets so big that you have to play football stadiums? What happens when you lose the connection you'd normally have in a smaller venue?*

What happens?

Nothing happens.

Your fans pay for the ticket, they go to the concert, you perform, and you make lots and lots of money. Shut the fuck up.

So the Who embarked on their Farewell Tour in the fall of 1982, and although I knew all about them, I hadn't really gotten into them. It wasn't that I didn't like them, I had the utmost respect for them just knowing who they were, no pun intended. I knew they were legends, but I just hadn't gotten the chance to get their albums and listen to their music beyond the obvious select songs that were played on the local FM rock stations WPLJ and WNEW. On the night of December 17, 1982, they ended it in Toronto. And that's exactly where I began. I was in Elizabeth, New Jersey, sleeping at my grandparent's house, and for some reason, turned in for bed a little on the early side for a Friday night. Just before ten o'clock as I was getting into my pajamas, I turned on the clock radio sitting beside the bed and tuned into WPLJ where Judas Priest's "You've Got Another Thing Comin'" was playing. I jumped around the room playing air guitar. By the end of the song, I was no longer tired, and as the hour began, the station entered into the world's very first satellite broadcast of a live rock concert that went out simultaneously on the radio and large screens in movie theaters. The Who were about to play their very last concert ever, and it was going out live on the radio...in real time as it happened. At around 10:10 PM Eastern Time, the Who took the stage, slamming into "My Generation." I was immediately transformed, and decided then and there that I was going to get into the Who. Me being the anal obsessive person that I am went into the kitchen to grab a pencil and some paper and brought it back to the bedroom where I tried to write down the setlist as the band played it. I successfully wrote down the first three songs either because I knew them, or they announced the title (My Generation, I Can't Explain, Dangerous), but by the fourth song, "Sister Disco," which I didn't know, I wrote it down as "The Disco Song." Of course "Baba O'Riley" was written as "Teenage Wasteland," and little mistakes like this happened throughout the night as I tried my 12-year old best to capture the Who's set on paper, so I'd know which songs to look for in the record store. For the songs that I didn't know, I listened as closely to the lyrics as I could just to leave myself the best description I could. Initially I heard "Boris the Spider" as "Horace the Spider" so that's what I wrote down. I knew "Long Live Rock" from the radio, but only knew it as "Rocky's Dead," only to later find out that Roger Daltrey was actually saying "Rock is dead."

Rock is dead, I thought.

Yeah, right.

The 1980s moved along with the underlying understanding that we'd never get to see bands like the Who or the Rolling Stones live again. And with regard to the biggest bands and artists of the previous two decades not firing on all cylinders, it wasn't exclusive to the 1960s acts. Seventies bands like Cheap Trick, ELO, Yes, Boston, Styx, and the Cars had either broken up, had an uncharacteristic commercial hit song or two and disappeared...or just disappeared without even that much. Artists like Billy Joel and Elton John who had done their grittiest, streetwise music in the previous decade had mellowed into the most unremarkable periods of their recording careers. David Bowie had a monster hit album in 1983, but spent the rest of the decade spiraling into the most irrelevant run of consecutive albums of his career. By the mid-Eighties, even Paul McCartney hit a bit of a dry patch. Acts that cohesively held the decade together even if it constituted patchwork were Bruce Springsteen, Prince, Michael Jackson and Madonna along with a bunch of much smaller bands and artists and one-hit wonders. The Eighties were the decade of the American artist. The way British bands had dominated the previous decade and a half, American artists dominated the Eighties. But then again, that's always been the overall case throughout the history of rock music. Britain had the better bands and America had the better artists. Britain gave us the Beatles, the Rolling Stones, the Who, Led Zeppelin, Pink Floyd, the Kinks, the Clash, etc... America gave us Elvis Presley, Chuck Berry, Bob Dylan, Bruce Springsteen, Michael Jackson, and Prince. Of course, there are always exceptions in both cases. David Bowie or R.E.M. anyone?

Enter 1989.

At the beginning of the last year of the decade, things began to turn around ever so slightly...and just enough to give you the sense that maybe everything we thought to be concrete and absolute wasn't in fact written in stone. The year began with Lou Reed releasing *New York*, his best album in 16 years, although some critics spoke favorably about 1982's *The Blue Mask*. The sudden appearance of *New York* however, coinciding with a run of shows at the St, James Theatre was treated as a major cultural event. In April, the Who announced a reunion tour to mark their twenty-fifth anniversary, which in itself would have made the year memorable for me personally. In August, the Stones announced a new album and their first tour in seven years. So by that fall, I had gotten to see two bands live that I never imagined I would have the chance to see. The final season of the 1980s also saw the release of the monumental *Oh Mercy* album by Bob Dylan. He began what would become known as the Never Ending Tour a year earlier after releasing the yawnfest, *Down in the Groove*. Since he was a year into that tour by the early fall of 89, with more shows planned, *Oh Mercy* seemed to have come out of nowhere. Truth is, he was as busy as he'd ever been. Releasing *Down in the Groove*, beginning a tour while simultaneously juggling Traveling Wilburys sessions, and managing to travel back and forth to New Orleans to record a new album with producer, Daniel Lanois between shows throughout 1989. *Oh Mercy* showed up unexpectedly and was met with the most critical praise Dylan had received since 1975's *Blood on the Tracks*. My love for *Oh Mercy* was instant, and I drew immediate controversy amongst my Dylan fan friends who all fell in line with the universally-accepted belief that *Blood on the Tracks* was the best album Dylan did after *Blonde on Blonde*...this idea that assigns the album a masterpiece status that equals *Blonde on Blonde* and the undeniable greatness and grandiosity of everything Dylan did up through 1966. To this day, every time Dylan releases a good album, critics en masse all gather round it to praise it as "his best since *Blood On The Tracks*." And we all know that *Blood On The Tracks* has always his best album since *Blonde On Blonde*.

Or is it?

To deny it is sacrilege. But my biggest personal philosophy on music criticism is that we need to remain objective about our favorite artists. And that's why I don't mind committing a little sacrilege here and there. The two biggest clichés of Dylan criticism are "Dylan is Back" and "his best album since *Blood on the Tracks*." We've heard both several times each decade.

The truth as I see it is *Blood On The Tracks* is too revered for its own good, and every other great Dylan album's own good as well (post-*Blood*, of course). I don't dare say "overrated," because the first four songs alone make it the masterpiece it is. Still, nobody seems to consider the masterpiece it *isn't*, while many tend to overlook one very important detail...and that's that everything great about *Blood* happens in the first four songs. "Tangled Up in Blue," "Simple Twist of Fate," You're a Big Girl Now" and "Idiot Wind" all make *Blood on the Tracks* the album it is known as. "Shelter From the Storm" to a large degree lives up to the same masterful shades of melancholy brilliance. But what happens after the first 18 minutes once "Idiot Wind" comes to an end? "You're Gonna Make Me Lonesome When You Go" and "If You See Her Say Hello," while nice in a sentimental sort of way are no better than some of the great material on *Planet Waves* or even *New Morning. Planet Waves* contains material that is just as powerful as most of *Blood* ("Wedding Song," "Dirge"). But that's nitpicking. What really ruins *Blood* is the immeasurable hole in the middle formed by "Meet Me in the Morning" and "Lily, Rosemary and the Jack of Hearts"...two songs that completely castrate the consistency of mood created in the first half of the record. "Meet Me in the Morning" does not live up to half of what the previous songs are. It is an inferior color-by-numbers piece of blues filler...worthy only of an album like *Self Portrait* or Columbia's 1973 revenge piece, *Dylan*. "Lily," on the surface, sounds like a silly and clumsy piece of drunken polka before Dylan even opens his mouth. Once the lyrics start and the unattractive music shows no sign of letting up, it sounds a lot less like a great Dylan song than it does something from Billy Joel's Los Angelinos period. While it is true these two songs are adored by people, they are never mentioned in relation to the album's greatness...nor should they be.

This hardly makes for a masterpiece let alone a great album. Still, *Blood* manages to get away with that reputation. Why? Because despite this, it still *is* a great album. but it's the whole "It's his best album since *Blood on the Tracks*" cliche that we've been hearing a few times each decade since *Slow Train Coming*, which makes me more and more vocal with each new album about how there are several better albums than *Blood*...namely *Oh Mercy* and *Love and Theft*...both of which imperious from beginning to end. Granted, *Oh Mercy* has the throwaway "Everything's Broken," but when you have "Most of the Time," "What Was it You Wanted," "Ring them Bells," "What Good am I," "Man in the Long Black Coat" and "Shooting Star" all on the same album, "Everything's Broken" is easily forgiven. Again, "Tangled" through "Idiot Wind" allow *Blood* its legendary status. It is also arguable that none of those aforementioned *Oh Mercy* songs really touch *Blood*'s first four songs, but there is also an argument to be made that they are *as good.* Because *Blood* was recorded in two different cities during two radically different sets of sessions, we can almost pinpoint what doesn't belong with what. The rude 13-minute interruption right down the middle of *Blood* ruins any chance of cohesion in the whole of the final product... and cohesion is one of the most important elements of a great album... and *Oh Mercy* in its gorgeosity and profound universality is far more consistent and cohesive than *Blood On The Tracks* ever was. Anything magical that starts to happen on side one is derailed by inferior songs, and "Shelter" aside, it barely recovers.

Could it be that Bob only had five masterpieces and had to fill out the rest with lesser material? Not lesser material in the sense that "Pledgin My Time" is less than "Visions of Johanna," but *far* lesser material? Are those five songs perfect and the rest just *great*? *Good? Mediocre?* Or does that other material on the album in anyone's eyes or ears even touch those five songs? Is the album really the untouchable masterpiece that so many Dylan fans and critics make it out to be? Let's of course recognize that there are lots of fans who genuinely love every song on *Blood on the Tracks*. That is not the point. But there are also people who are blindly loyal to it while staying in denial of it. It's kind of like knowing mobsters personally once they've gotten into your life...you either love them or pretend to love them...but you also fear crossing them. All the Dylan freaks I know are shit-scared of *Blood on the Tracks*, and they act as though someone or something is going to strike them down if they dare question how great it *really* is. A great album, no question...but its "best post-*Blonde On Blonde*" status is badly in need of reassessment. To be fair, *Blood* is a masterpiece... but it's when I refer to it as a "flawed masterpiece" that gets me in trouble with the people who refuse to question its status. Whatever the case, this book is not the appropriate vessel to hold a review of the *Oh Mercy* album, but in reference to 1989, the year I'm attempting to convey, the album requires mention simply because Dylan, once again, was back...and he had created his best album since *Blood on the Tracks*. And that's why he was back. Every time the best album since *Blood on the Tracks* was released, it warranted the big return for journalists and critics. And so, in 1989, Bob Dylan was back.

And so was Ringo Starr. While the ex-Beatle drummer had never really garnered much critical praise of his solo work, he was still a Beatle, and that meant everything when it was announced that he was going on tour. No Beatle had been on tour in the States since the mid-Seventies, so the chance for my generation to actually see a Beatle was a first. Starr assembled what he called his All Star Band comprised of himself, Joe Walsh, Nils Lofgren, Dr. John, Billy Preston, Rick Danko, Levon Helm, Clarence Clemons and Jim Keltner. Over the next few decades, the band would take on a few dozen more members and guests as it became a celebration of talent without any set concrete lineup. Ringo Starr, a Beatle, was back on the road in 1989.

And so was Paul McCartney. The subtext to McCartney's late 1989 effort, *Flowers in the Dirt*, was actually the true headline. The ex-Beatle was going to tour the States again for the first time since 1976. Let's be clear in these astonishing facts. While the Beatles are undoubtedly by far the most popular band in the history of pop music, most people never got a chance to see them live. Their touring history from touching down at JFK to Candlestick Park only spanned two and a half years, so those who got to see them were the only ones who got to see them. For the anal retentive, I fully acknowledge the band's existence pre-February of 1964, but let's face it...there's the story and there's the Story. The story begins in Liverpool, but the Story begins in America and without America, there's no Story. So while most people didn't get to see the Beatles, the Baby Boomers finally got a chance to see McCartney in 1976 when he toured with Wings. People had had prior chances to see other Beatles with sporadic performances or brief appearances from John Lennon, George Harrison, and Ringo Starr, mostly in New York City, while Harrison had done an entire tour in 1974 to scathing reviews due to his Hare Krishna thing. McCartney, the favorite Beatle of many, at long last went out on the road in 1976, and by 1989, had not been on tour since, with the exception of a brief UK run in 1979. That however, was not uncommon. None of the Beatles had really been in the public eye aside from the occasional new album release. Harrison, after 1974 would never tour again. Lennon who continued to have albums released in his name although not to his knowledge, could not tour because he was dead. So when McCartney trekked across the States for the first time in 13 years, it was yet another chance for the Boomers to see him if they had missed it in 76 or perhaps 66. And it was the first chance for my generation to see him at all (unless you were a toddler seeing him on the Wings tour). It is quite something to think how I graduated high school believing that era of rock and roll was a thing of the past and that these guys in their mid-forties were maybe too old to do it anymore, while lamenting over the thought that I would never get to see any of them except maybe

Dylan or the Grateful Dead who never really seemed to go away. Two years later, I saw the Who, the Rolling Stones, and two Beatles.

1989.

Even Neil Young returned to fiery vitality by way of a new album called *Freedom*. After a decade of experimentation with synth pop, new wave, rockabilly and country, *Freedom* reached back to the sound of 1979's *Rust Never Sleeps,* balancing melodic acoustic ballads in minor keys and raucous pre-grunge. In the same way that *Rust* was bookended by acoustic and electric versions of "My My Hey Hey" and "Hey Hey My My," *Freedom* was bookended by acoustic and electric versions of a new song called "Rockin' in the Free World," which held a mirror to a worldwide American reputation ravaged by the Reagan era and the beginning of the Bush post-script.

The 1980s decade was the Baby Boomers in their late thirties and early forties. It was the 1960s counterculture generation coming to terms with not just adulthood (that came somewhat earlier), but with the knowledge that their way of life, the work they did through music and art and the mark they left may not always be relevant and may actually at some point be considered passé. Some such as Townshend believed this to be true early in the decade, which is why he took the Who off the road and ended the band as a recording entity. By decade's end, most musical midlife crises had come to an end and a new era had been born where these artists would enter the next decade as elder statesmen. The term *classic rock* would seep into pop culture looked upon suspiciously, but eventually become a legitimate label, wrapped in reverence initially, although some despised hearing those words together...and gradually losing recognition with youth as the twenty-first century would send it all to plunge inevitably down into the compartmentalized categories of *dinosaur* and *grandfather* music. Several years into the 1990s, we'd see the awakening of even more acts of rock's second generation. Jimmy Page and Robert Plant would reunite to play Zeppelin music and even record an album of new material under the name Plant/Page. The Jefferson Airplane would reform without Grace Slick and the Kinks and Pink Floyd would return. Even Steely Dan, a mysterious ever-changing outfit of studio musicians with only two official members, Donald Fagan and Walter Becker holding it together over the years without having toured since 1974, would assemble an actual band again that would hit the arena circuit to much demand and success. The Eagles would play again after 14 years. We'd watch these artists cross over into their fifties and it would be unprecedented in rock and roll. With that obvious exception of those we'd lost, many were still very present on the scene and it was very easy to take that for granted. Within another decade or two, they'd be that much older, and the uncertainty of the future of rock would be that much more a reality.

And then came the dinosaurs.

Given that this sentiment has largely occurred during the first two decades of the third millennium, it is rather safe to say that as rock fans, there were several things we just never considered would happen:

One, that our rock music, whether it be Sixties, Seventies, or even Eighties, would one day no longer be the center of the world. The world would no longer revolve around rock and its glorious, celebratory, hedonistic, culture-informed self. What we once thought to be concrete, absolute and eternal would run its course and fizzle out.

Two, the era we speak of would become just that...an era...and fall into place within history like anything else that gets classified as an *era* or a *period*, involuntarily lying down to accept its inevitable fate of becoming irrelevant and obsolete to the next few generations and beyond. Historical significance notwithstanding, it would no longer have a stake in the future and vice versa.

And three, nobody would care.

How arrogant and self-important each generation is to insist theirs is the end-all-be-all...the absolute optimum of any given subject or situation. Each generation, however, is on the cutting edge. After all, we're moving forward, not backwards. There is only right now, the present, and the present at any given time in history is as far as technology has come, politics has come, sports has come, and the arts have come until the present becomes the past and the next generation pushes it all even further. But does the passage of time necessarily always mean progress? Do periods of stagnation exist? And to what extent can the answers to such questions be subjective?

A song that lends itself in some small fashion to these thoughts is Billy Joel's "We Didn't Start the Fire." It climbed the charts during the last months of 1989. It traced a mere 40 years of history as seen through the eyes of the Baby Boom generation...a generation, again, coming to terms with its own mortality and possible irrelevance to the big picture. By no fucking means did they start the fire. It was burning long before them, and it will burn long after them. Same goes for my generation. But from my own personal viewpoint, much closer to Generation X than to the Boomers, I didn't philosophize and break it down to such a level in analysis as I sat in my car in the parking lot of Metro Park Train Station hearing the song for the first time on the radio. All I thought was *hey Billy Joel is back with a new album!*

And while my friends and I (possibly a microcosm of the larger concern for the state of rock and roll throughout the rest of the world) often lamented about the state of rock music at the time, along with the drought of anything significant happening, we still spoke about good things ahead in the future. We didn't know the *what*, *when*, or *who*, but we knew that rock was going to get better. We had many of our classic artists active and vital again. Were *they* going to lead the charge into the future? What did the 1990s have in store for us? Would it take the old and decrepit bands now in their late forties to turn it all around and give it the swift kick in the ass it so desperately needed? Or would something totally new and unexpected shake up the rock world in its own modern day revolution?

Back in the present day for a moment, we assess the barren landscape of music, devoid of much originality. Without harping on the synthetic, airtight sound of the twenty-first century and soulless Autotune that would-be artists rely on, I can't help but be reminded of two critically-acclaimed albums that were released in consecutive years 2014 and 2015. One was called *1989*, and the other was called *1989*. The first *1989* was done by Taylor Swift, one of the more respected and prolific artists to come out of the new millennium. Unlike most of her millennial peers, Swift actually writes most of her songs and knows how to play actual instruments. There is enough talent to insure that unlike most of those millennial peers, she was not processed and manufactured in a lab. Swift named the album *1989* after the year she was born, as well as the pop music that supposedly inspired it from that same year. That, however, is where it ends. While the songs have some artistic value within today's compromised musical standards, none of it remotely resembles the sound of 1989. With respect to Swift, the biggest pop music of that year was breaking color and religious taboos with political and social undercurrents driving the motivation of artists. Madonna's *Like a Prayer* and Janet Jackson's *Rhythm Nation 1814* come to mind. But even considering a host of other pop acts that released albums that year...Prince, Richard Marx, Gloria Estefan, Stacy Q, Jody Watley, Debbie Gibson, Neneh Cherry, Tears For Fears, Taylor Dayne, Terrance Trent D'Arby, Queen Latifah, Milli Vanilli or Technotronic... as brilliant, disposable or fraudulent as some of it was, it was still recorded in an era that could deliver a somewhat organic sound and feel to a pop song...something that could never be comprehended by the people behind the production of today's records. That *1989* won the Grammy for *album of the year* is far more telling of the state of music today than of Swift's album. Like her other albums, it's a collection of break up songs that so inspired one of the other respected artists of current times, Ryan Adams to remake the entire album song-for-song just one year later. Adams's version of *1989* bears little resemblance to Swift's, and again, the supposed inspiration for the album other than the year of Swift's birth, has no weight on either project. So it is in name only that these millennial *1989* albums come to mind when reflecting on the real 1989. Long before 1989 became a punch line, the real 1989 looked and sounded much different. And it *was* much different. *Things* were happening.

5

THE SUMMER OF LOVE AND HATE

Uptight assholes have always tried to cancel artists straight back to the very beginnings of rock and roll. The racist pre-Civil Rights South tried to cancel Elvis Presley by smashing his records because, well, they thought he was corrupting all the white kids with his black music. Self-righteous Christians tried to cancel the Beatles when John Lennon stated the obvious...that his band was more popular with kids in 1966 than Jesus Christ was. They tried to cancel Kiss for being "knights in Satan's service." They tried to cancel Ozzy if he so much as farted...I mean the poor guy could do nothing right without conservatives breathing down his neck in the 1980s. Roseanne Barr? They tried to cancel her long before she was actually cancelled decades later. The first time was when some people didn't like how she sang the national anthem at a baseball game. We can cite examples of outrage up and down the entire modern pop era. The difference between past and present is that cancelations never worked back then. Careers and lives weren't ruined every time someone took offense to something or had to point a finger in order to blame someone for something. Artists went on with their lives and were still allowed to have a career. None of it was motivated by politics and it was before FOX News pundits were around to instigate boycotts and death threats. When I say none of it was political, I exclude the political right's hatred of John Lennon and the Nixonian surveillance John had to balance with all the rest of his problems. They didn't want to *cancel* John. They just wanted him out of America. The politics that dictated FOX's encouragement of cancelation every time someone like Bruce Springsteen voiced an opinion or the fallout they provided for the Dixie Chicks when Natalie Maines spoke out against an illegal war were far different, and it was politics that became the template that informed how conservatives in America treated the First Amendment rights of musical artists and actors in Hollywood. In other words, people like Springsteen, Sean Penn and Eddie Vedder would get crucified for the same thing Ted Nugent, Scott Baio and Kid Rock got applauded for... simply because the latter artists somehow ended up as conservatives. The division and hypocrisy was never this deep before FOX News. But FOX News didn't exist in 1992...and in the fall of that year, something very disturbing happened to alter the landscape of an artist's First Amendment rights...even if it took the conservative right wing another decade before it realized that people can indeed be cancelled. Oddly enough, it happened at a concert celebrating the most significant voice of the counterculture...and possibly the biggest artist whose music was a backdrop to the overall liberal cause.

I'm standing in one of the stalls of a men's room on the 200 level of Madison Square Garden with my penis in my hand. It's Friday night,

October 16, 1992, and I'm witnessing history. I'm drunk but still very aware of the significance of the evening and all I am taking in. From the farthest reaches of the Garden, I can hear the echoing sounds of the Clancy Brothers making their way through Bob Dylan's "When the Ship Comes In." The sound bounces off every rafter and section wall, ricocheting across the arena and beyond, as it becomes cushioned and muffled by the time it reaches the halls and even farther, the restrooms. I'm usually pee-shy and prefer to avoid urinals whenever I can. So in the stall I stand. I've been holding it in all night, having waited through one exciting act after another. In the past few hours, I've seen Stevie Wonder, John Mellencamp, Tom Petty, Lou Reed, Johnny Cash, June Carter Cash, Rosanne Cash, Booker T and the MGs, Eddie Vedder, Tracy Chapman, Richie Havens, Ron Wood, Mary Chapin Carpenter, George Thorogood, Willie Nelson, Johnny Winter and Kris Kristofferson. They're all paying tribute to Bob Dylan on the thirtieth anniversary of his signing with Columbia Records. I was hoping, even praying for an act that I had no interest in seeing, just so I could get up and pee. It was at the arrival of the Clancy Brothers onto the stage where I jumped out of my seat, left Tom and Eric, and headed for the aisles. As I recount this story and send it back into past tense, let me once again veer off track into an underlying subtext that accompanies this particular story. In the weeks leading up to this particular event, one that was heavily promoted and talked about with intense anticipation on rock radio, it became widely speculated upon whether or not Bruce Springsteen was going to be there. As reality would have it, Bruce was on tour and scheduled for a show in Washington State that night. Yet, rumors persisted of the Boss cancelling his gig to quickly fly across the country from the opposite coast to pay tribute to one of his biggest influences. There were rumors of Mick Jagger and Keith Richards showing up as well...but for me personally, the hope was that somehow by some miracle, Bruce would show up. So, as I walked through the halls of the Garden toward the nearest men's room, I could hear the sounds of the Clancy Brothers performing "When the Ship Comes In," and so could lots of other people who made their way toward some other form of arena civilization aside from watching the Clancy Brothers perform "When the Ship Comes In." Assorted stragglers in various forms of intoxication squantered up, down, across and around the narrow corridors of the Garden in search of food, drink, or a place to pee. A designated smoking area was not one of those destinations, as this was before you had to go outside near the escalators to smoke. Smoking was still allowed in the Garden in 1992, so it was one less inconvenience. But I had to pee, so to the men's room I went, and as I walked in, I was pleasantly surprised by the vast emptiness where only one or two people were up against urinals. Still, I chose a stall and was finally able to unleash the torrent of the last three hours of beers. As I stood there drunkenly swaying back and forth trying to direct the flow as best I could without creating a fucking disaster, I laughed to myself at the thought of what an amazing and mind-blowing night I was having, and of all the legendary artists I was seeing. Damn, I thought. I had just seen Johnny Cash! And Stevie Wonder! And George Harrison was still coming up...another Beatle that I would get to be in the same room with! What a night it had been and still was!

As I stood at the bowl watching the final broken streams of pee trickle down into the water, it had become apparent to me that some point during my deep contemplation of the night, the Clancy Brothers performance had come to an end and the background noise was reduced to a distant applause. The final pee trickled out. I watched it. The applause began to die down. Something deep within my drunken state had suppressed the urge to want to get back to my seat in order to see who the next act was for fear I might miss something. I had gotten complacent in the stall and just stood for a few seconds watching the broken flow turn to eventual isolated drops. Staring down into the toilet, I lost focus as my stare morphed into complete zoning.

And then I heard it.

At first it was as unpronounced as white noise, not fully getting my attention...until I realized what it was.

It was a vowel sound.

"Bruuuuuuuuuuuuuce!"

I looked up, startled!

The distant roar of the crowd.

"Bruuuuuuuuuuuuuce!" they screamed!

Fuck!

"Bruuuuuuuuuuuuuuuuuuuuuuuuuuuuuuce!"

I let go of the band of my briefs as it snapped back, pinning my dick flat against the surface of skin beneath my belly button, the head sticking out from the top of my underwear like the gopher in *Caddyshack* peeking out of the hole in the ground.

Fuck!

I put everything back in place, zipped my jeans, and ran out of the men's room.

"Fuck!" I screamed, booking through the slender and confined trails of the Garden, feeling as though I were on a treadmill and getting nowhere. I was furious and panicking at the same time. I sat there the entire night...and the one time I get up to pee, Bruce shows up. Typical! *Fucking typical!*

As I got closer to my section, the crowd roar grew louder and more intense. *God fucking damnit! He's onstage already,* I'm thinking. *I've missed his whole introduction!*

"BRUUUUUUUUUUUUUUUUUUCE!"

I approached my section and walked in where I was eventually able to see the circular shape of the ceiling as I got closer to being inside. As I came up between sections walking inside, the screen hanging from the ceiling over the middle of the Garden floor became visible, and nothing could have prepared me for what I saw, and for what was actually taking place. And it sure wasn't Bruce Springsteen. On the screen was the face of Sinead O'Connor in full close-up. The camera then panned back to reveal her standing onstage, arms at her side, face looking down. And the Bruce chants were not Bruce chants, but boos. Loud relentless boos. Sinead had ripped up a picture of Pope John Paul II on *Saturday Night Live* about a week earlier. A while back, she refused to go onstage in Holmdel, New Jersey because the venue played the national anthem before each show. Indeed, she had ruffled some feathers as of late, so on the surface it wasn't surprising that they booed her. What blew my mind though, was that it was at an event for Bob Dylan. This was an audience made up of people who had protested the Vietnam War. It was an audience that had stood up and protested for civil rights, women's rights, gay rights and social justice across the board. So, when Sinead was protesting the silence of the Catholic Church in the face of child abuse or the sexually abusive actions of many a Catholic priest, or protesting oppression by not wanting nationalist sentiment imposed on her performance, it probably should have registered to the children of the 1960s that this was an extension of their counterculture. Instead, they booed. Not all did. Most applauded. But the booing no question drowned out the applause at first. I stood there frozen in the aisle, unable to move. My eyes shifted back and forth from Sinead's image on the screen to the stage where I could see her actual tiny frail figure standing there. She just stood in place, taking in a monstrous wall of shouts and boos all around her. I was witnessing a massive public condemnation of one human being, and it was both surreal and frightening. It reminded me of one of those scenes of ancient Rome where a gladiator or slave standing in the middle of the Colosseum is being shouted down or condemned with a cheering crowd calling for death. I thought of Jesus at the moment the Jews chose Barabbas. The overzealous screaming surrounding one central figure had to have been similar. I'd never witnessed anything like this and it wasn't what I signed on for when I bought my ticket. Regardless of how you felt about Sinead at the time, it was a scary and ugly scene. Between the cheers and the boos, it was an overbearing clash of sound unlike anything I'd ever heard at a concert. I'd heard similar sounds at football games, but never such collective and sustained disapproval at such a volume.

Sinead O'Connor stood onstage at Madison Square Garden waiting for the crowd noise to die down so she could begin her performance of Bob Dylan's "I Believe in You." The crowd, however, would not let her. She was there to pay tribute to Dylan...and the crowd, his fans, would not let her begin. The booing was relentless. After two minutes of nonstop cheers and jeers, the keyboard player began the song, probably hoping people would settle down...but Sinead immediately cut him off, motioning for him to stop. She then ripped out her ear monitor and told the sound guy to turn up the mic. Seconds later, she ripped into an a cappella version of Bob Marley's "War," the same song she had performed on *SNL*. This time she bellowed out the lyrics, determined to get above the volume of the crowd. The defiant look in her eyes seemed to have come as a result of possibly being appalled by half the audience's hostile reaction. It was almost as if she were thinking *this is what happens in America if you speak out against pedophilia and child abuse? Fuck you all!* She shot the crowd one more disapproving stare upon finishing the song and walked offstage where Kris Kristofferson stood by to greet her in an embrace. Sinead hurried off behind him however, cupping her mouth as if she were going to vomit on him. The crowd roared in satisfaction as if delighted that they had shaken her up enough to run off the stage. At that instance, I realized that I had been standing in place between seating sections for about three minutes, and continued walking back toward my seat. When I reached my row, Tom and Eric were looking at me in shock as if to say *Holy shit... What the hell just happened?*

I sat in my seat...stunned. I couldn't believe what I'd just seen take place. I was so consumed by the thought of it that it wasn't until halfway through Neil Young's second song that I even realized Neil Young was playing. I missed most of Neil's set and he was right in front of me the entire time.

I wasn't a humongous fan of Sinead O'Connor at the time. I had her first album and thought it was pretty damn good, but never followed up with the other two albums she had. "Jerusalem" and "Just Like You

Said it Would Be" were really great songs that I played pretty often, but again, I hadn't kept up with her other records. That said, I was taken aback by the audience's reaction to her in the sense that...one, here was an artist standing up to injustices in ways that were absolutely traditional in the chain of rock and roll activism that went all the way back to Woody Guthrie. And two, it was a Dylan audience...children of the counterculture and their children. Hippies. Anti-establishment motherfuckers whose M.O. was sticking it to the man. One of their own would be elected president of the United States in less than one month.

What was going on here?

How could this happen?

How could they boo?

Almost everyone on the stage that night had something in their blood, in their DNA, in their artistic heritage and output that at least left traces of pissing off the establishment in one way or the other. In retrospect, it was probably the first crack in the foundation of what was once the rebellious spirit of rock and roll. It marked a softening in tone and a corruption of values as a major part of a symbolic era chose to be offended over the actions of an artist rather than recognize and appreciate the human, social and artistic integrity in it. Sinead's actions certainly garnered negative attention in recent weeks, but coming from a generation of hippies, the booing was almost as offensive and disgusting an act as many found her actions to be.

But were they all hippies? Were they even Baby Boomers? Were most of them even Bob Dylan fans? These were questions asked in all forums of discussion in the days and weeks following the event. Suddenly, the socio-economic implications surrounding the show came into focus as it became apparent from fans having been there, that it was a gathering of suits of all kinds gobbling up the majority of the astronomically-priced tickets...CEOs, investment bankers, sports team owners, big business galore enjoying the benefits of first dibs. Within a few more years, as triple digit ticket prices became the norm, it would become customary for promoters to offer the best seats to the rich before tickets became available to the plebian public.

A simple comparison of the before and after of this period of time: It used to be that we'd hear of a concert, and wait for the ticket information. When tickets went on sale, we stood on a line at Ticketron or Ticketmaster. If they expected extremely long lines, we were given a wristband the day before, which only guaranteed you a place on line, but not always a ticket. Still, everyone had a shot at a ticket, and everyone had a shot at great seats. By the mid to late-Nineties, when a show went on sale, the first week was only open to the holders of the American Express Gold Card. The rest of us had to read about the Golden Circle seats or whatever-the-fuck else it was that we peasants couldn't afford. And even if we could, we weren't part of that club, so we had to wait for the shitty seats to become available, for which we'd still have to pay three times what we were paying just five years earlier. In 1986, Gordon Gecko uttered the arrogant line that became the catch phrase of the Reagan Eighties, "Greed is good." By the mid-Nineties, that greed reached rock and roll.

As concerts became excuses for very expensive social gatherings, the sacramental experience for diehard fans became watered down and cheapened as prices went through the roof. To explain this thought in more detail, I will give two examples drawn from actual conversations that occurred between 1999 and 2003. The first took place on the golf course of a country club in Central Jersey on the afternoon of Wednesday, July 14, 1999:

Mr. Ashkeeshkenshkeez: *Alright I gotta head back to the office...Connie is meeting me there with my grandson. Tell Twiggy I'll pass on the hot dog when he gets back.*

Roberts: *(laughs) okay, will do*

Mr. A: *Oh, by the way, Connie's got a...some extra tickets to see the ah... ahh...that Bruce Springstreet tomorrow. What are you and your wife doing tomorrow? Ya wanna come?*

Roberts: *Uh...I can't stand him but Sheila's firm was given 24 tickets and I'm already stuck going on Saturday.*

The second conversation happened in the break room of an insurance company in January 2003:

Jennifer: *Oh my God, Matt got us tickets for La Vesta De Zortda.*

Heather: *What the heck is that?*

Jennifer: *I'm not really sure. I think it's an opera.*

Heather: *You like opera that much? You seem excited.*

Jennifer: *I don't know. It'll be something different.. ya know?*

Heather: *David and I are going to see the Rolling Stones in New York on the 17th.*

Jennifer: *Wait. You guys got tickets?*

Heather: *Yeah, we're going with some guys from his company.*

Jennifer: *Heather, we have like a dozen tickets for that show.*

Heather: *You and Matt?*

Jennifer: *No, us! The company! You know we get tickets for every concert. You could have gone with us.*

Heather: *Oh, I don't know. I don't even care for the Rolling Stones that much. Matt's just going because they talk business at these things and it's just a place to go. They do it all the time at the Knicks and Rangers games. I mean it's the Stones and all, and I do like some of their really early stuff. What that's song they have? You can start me up? That was one of their first songs when they first came out in the 80s. I liked that song.*

So, it's people like Heather, Matt, Roberts and Mr. Ashkeeshkensh-keez...people who don't really care about music who have to fuck it up for the real fans who just want to go and see their favorite band or artist. Yet, the majority of the tickets go to non-appreciative imposters in suits. Unaccountable assfucks who without thinking twice would hold a meeting on the upcoming fiscal year at a Roger Waters performance of *The Wall* just as easily as they would in the food court of the World Financial Center.

Honestly, I was disturbed by the booing of Sinead O'Connor at the Dylan tribute. This was an audience that had burned their draft cards in the 1960s. Even if we rule out all the martini assholes, it was still largely a crowd of Dylan fans who knew exactly what Bob Dylan was about, even if Bob Dylan had never said so himself.

Wasn't it?

These were thinkers inside the Garden that night...humanists... social justice advocates...hippies...

Suits.

Investment bankers.

Yuppies.

Conservatives.

Offended.

The cheers would eventually rise to drown out the boos...and that's where the Dylan fans who knew better stood in defense of Sinead... cheering...shouting down the stuffed shirt infiltration. But it was too late. America's Puritan lineage was hard to hide in the cavernous venue as it surfaced and bubbled its way to a finger-pointing head.

At what point did half a generation get the granddaddy of all sticks up its ass? If there had been anything noble about music in the 1980s, it's the fact that it had become more socially and politically active than ever, along with consciousness-raising. The 1960s counterculture was coming full circle, and its influence and spirit was seen in everything from U2 to REM to *USA For Africa* to Live Aid to Janet Jackson to Public Enemy. Earlier in the year, a massive rock and roll revolution happened, ignited by MTV catching up with some underground music that would prove vital and relevant to its own time. The media had to hang a label on it as they do with everything, so they called it grunge. In the fall of 1991, Nirvana's "Smells Like Teen Spirit" appeared on Music Television near its last days of actually playing music, and blah blah blah, we know the rest. By the summer of 1992, we'd seen the rebirth of the long-lost festival in the form of Lollapolooza, then in its second year. The radio playlists as well as MTV's were rock and grunge-heavy. There were also equal parts rap and R&B to strike a harmonious balance of co-existence not seen in music since. If you were of Generation X, 1992 was your 1967. It was our playground. In rock, there was a blurred residency among bands and fans alike, made up of hippies, punks, rappers and metalheads...all interweaving as closely as they ever did or ever would again. And while not everything was quite a peaceable kingdom as the strains and echoes of the Los Angeles riots still reverberated throughout the States, it was as close to my generation's Summer of Love as well as the later tumult of 1968 as we would simultaneously get in our youth. Rock and roll and liberal democracy were flourishing. There also lay the promise of a Democrat from Arkansas, the first counterculture president who was about to pull the country out of twelve years of Gordon Gecko-style policies... an American president that would actually be seen as cool to Generation X while the Baby Boomers would finally have one of their own in the White House...only to be met eight years later with a conservative backlash that would profoundly make the world a much more dangerous place in the decades that followed. Little did we know of the civil unrest and chaotic times that lay ahead well into adulthood. For the time being, 1992 was our summer of love and hate. Whatever the case, there was a spirit of rebellion, social activism and political awareness in the air.

But out of nowhere, the brakes screeched inside the Garden and brought that spirit to a sudden halt. Sinead O'Connor declared war, walked offstage and left a bunch of us wondering what the hell had just happened.

6

THE RED SHOES AND THE BLUE ALBUM

There have often been events that I've looked forward to throughout my life that have been interrupted, thwarted or cancelled by some insane shit that happens. Two come to mind when I think of 1993. The one that I really won't get into was in late February when I was supposed to go see a children's production of *A Midsummer Night's Dream* somewhere in the west twenties of Manhattan. I had planned this with some girl named Alisande who was known around town for having a houseful of cats. I was never in her house and I never got to count them, but by most accounts, she had something like 50 cats in there. The story with her was that wherever she went, if she came across a cat on the street, she'd pick it up and take it home. She was literally a cat burglar. We never made it to the play, nor did we even attempt going into the city that Friday night because the bridges and tunnels were closed. Earlier in the day, the first World Trade Center bombing had taken place and Lower Manhattan was on lockdown. Ironically, my mom whose fear and contempt for New York City was well-known infiltrated the island by way of a limousine across the George Washington Bridge in order to attend a Gene Pitney concert at Carnegie Hall where the show went on as scheduled.

In early December of the same year, a man boarded a train car on the Long Island Railroad at Penn Station during rush hour. He sat through his ride for nearly 30 minutes. As the train approached a stop at Merillon Avenue in Garden City just after 6 PM, the man pulled out a 9-millimeter handgun, stood up and began walking down the aisle shooting people at random, ultimately killing six and injuring 19. To get an accurate picture of the public horror, it is necessary to remember that this incident took place years before mass shootings were an everyday normal part of desensitized American life. It can be difficult to fathom for some, but these kinds of shootings and mass murders were at one time shocking. Gun control was always on the minds of most sane people who didn't think mentally disturbed individuals should have such easy access to firearms, although it was already being politicized by gun nuts who blamed the train. Train safety and security became part of the talk that week and the reason I bring this up is because I had to get on a train to New York City two days later. Honestly, this was before I had a reliable car, so I was taking several trains into the city each week through my late teens and early twenties. I had become accustomed to trains, and although I hated riding them, I was quite comfortable on them most times. I also knew about probability, and I knew that I stood a much greater chance of having somebody's annoying kid sitting next to me. The last thing I was worried about was getting blown away by some asshole with a gun.

A week earlier, it was announced that Kate Bush would be appearing at the downtown Tower Records in New York City. The artist, musician and singer, already a legend at 35, was known for being a recluse, was rarely seen in public, and had only toured once...in 1978...a brief 6-week tour of Europe, never having played in the United States. And so, when I remember this event which is etched in my memory because of how monumental it seemed to me at the time, it often overshadows the tragic events that happened earlier in the week.

Thursday, December 9, 1993. I was never one for lines. Usually, I'm pretty patient when it comes to most things. Not lines. Whether I'm in a store, a restaurant, driving in traffic...anything really...I try to avoid them at all costs. I just don't do lines. But that's what I was faced with when I arrived on Great Jones Street between Broadway and Lafayette in the East Village. The entrance to Tower Records was around the block on Broadway and Fourth. The signing was for 4:30 that afternoon. I was already scheduled to meet Tom and our friend Sal for dinner across town at 6:30. Sal, our legendary English teacher, Mr. C, who we stayed in touch with past high school and had become good friends with, was going to introduce us to one of his friends from the U.K. who had flown in for the week. We'd all be meeting at Hunan Pan, our favorite Chinese restaurant that resided on the northeast corner of Hudson and Perry, and had steamed vegetable dumplings to die for. I figured I had plenty of time before I had to meet them, and that there wouldn't be a lot of people on the Kate Bush line if I got there by three. Major screw-up on my part. I grossly miscalculated my time and underestimated public interest in Kate Bush...realizing this is *Kate Fucking Bush* we're talking about. Did I really think I was just going to comfortably get on line 90 minutes before the doors open and casually wander up to Kate? With the trail of humans literally wrapped around the "building," basically amounting to four city blocks, it hit me that there was an enormous demand for her to return to performing, recording...anything, really. So I got on line. What the hell else was I going to do? I spoke to lots of fans who were far more into her than I was...and yet it was something I understood on the level of my avid history with names like Springsteen, Bob Dylan, Patti Smith or even my love of Kiss when I was a little kid. Be a devoted fan to any artist or band, and I may not be able to relate to your interest in said artist or band, but I can understand it. Anybody who loves music that much should be able to understand.

Great Jones and Lafayette isn't quite a shithole but it's not very picturesque to want to observe for 90 straight minutes standing in one spot before the line finally starts to move. And when things start to move, things just as quickly slow down. And that became the pattern over the next hour. The line moves ten feet. The line stops for ten minutes. The line moves ten more feet. The line stops for ten more minutes. The line moves ten more feet. The line stops for ten more minutes. The line moves ten more feet. The line stops for ten more minutes. The line moves ten more feet. The line stops for ten more minutes...

It had gotten dark about 20 minutes after Kate Bush began signing copies of her new album *The Red Shoes* inside a building on the northwest corner of a square block that I lingered on the southeast corner of...glancing impatiently at my watch. I had to be in the West Village in under an hour and people were starting to talk. What they were saying was that Kate would be leaving at seven and that our part of the line wouldn't even make it into the store to see her. I was still two blocks around from the store entrance and was beginning to question whether or not I should blow off the whole thing and head toward meeting my friends. I had nothing for Kate to sign even if I made it inside. I'd already purchased a copy of *The Red Shoes* on CD but didn't have it with me, nor was I going to get another one. I really thought it would be cool to meet her but I also knew realistically that I had very little chance from that far back on line. I also needed to split soon. Fuck it, I thought. I jumped off the line and didn't look back. I trotted swiftly up the street past everyone in front of me and turned the corner where the line was wrapped around the building. I looked at the hundreds of people all pressed against the side of the building as I walked past them, knowing I had made the right decision in leaving. There was no way in fuck that I was going to make it into that store.

As I got to the end of the block, I saw the Tower entrance and noticed people walking in who weren't on the line. It immediately raised the question: Is the store still open to regular customers who don't want to meet Kate Bush and just want to shop? Playing dumb, I walked up to the entrance but hesitated before I walked in. The first few people standing in line looked at me.

"What's the line for? Who's here?" I asked.

"Kate Bush is doing a signing," some girl said.

I gave her a polite nod indicating that I probably had no clue who she was talking about, and then I casually strolled into the store. I walked quick and determined as if I knew what I was looking for and just there to buy it. I had no idea of the layout of the store, but I kept moving toward the back. As I walked, I waited for someone to say something, but nobody did. The store was in fact opened to the public for shopping. Out of the corner of my eye, I could see the table where

Kate was. The line was on the left side of the store as you walked in, and was managed by some security and a velvet rope sectioning off the event from the rest of the regular functions of Tower Records.

I've learned over the years that if you look like you know exactly what you're doing, nobody will question you or give you shit when it comes to jumping a line. Give the impression that you're somebody important who is supposed to be there, and nobody will really think anything of it. I will say though, that the one time it didn't work was a few blocks north of where I was that day. About five years later in 1998, Tori Amos was playing an intimate warm-up gig at Irving Plaza just before embarking on her first arena tour. Ticketless, I walked up to John Norris of MTV on the street and struck up a conversation with him about the show and Tori's plans. At the outset of that brief chat, I was struck by how thin he was. He was almost the same build as me, and definitely looked bigger on TV. I mentioned how I usually got tickets off the street from a scalper, but nobody out there was selling for this particular gig. It really had been a hush-hush, quietly-announced, last minute thing, and if you got tickets, you got tickets. If not, you ended up asking John Norris to sneak you in, which I did.

"I don't think I can do that, sorry," he chuckled as he began walking in. He was probably let in because he was immediately recognized, but he did wear the necessary credentials around his neck like everyone else from the media. I wore nothing but a hemp necklace. I got behind him anyway and tried to walk as close to him as possible while looking down, not making facial contact with anyone. I got into the entrance foyer, making it past the first security guy, but just as I was steps away from entering the venue, a second guard grabbed me.

"Whoah, where you going? Let me see your ticket." Norris was no longer in sight, but I quickly pointed into the venue and turned around looking the guy square in the eyes while throwing up my hands in a "what the hell?" manner. It didn't work.

I walked up an aisle inside Tower and stopped at the Beatles CDs because they were close enough to where Kate Bush was sitting. There were about four cafeteria-like tables set up in a U shape surrounding her. She was dressed all in black as far as I could see, was tiny, and remarkably young-looking (35 at the time). She smiled a lot at everyone approaching her. I was there just to catch a glimpse, but something came over me that told me if I were ever to meet and talk to Kate Bush, now was the time. I stopped pretending to look at CDs and slowly wandered over toward the tables that were surrounding her. I stopped at the velvet rope but turned away from her to pretend I was looking at the Blue Album CDs. The Beatles matching red and blue greatest hits albums from 1973 had recently been released on CD after years of not being available. Don't forget: At this point in time, not every album in an artist or band's catalog had been issued on CD yet, and some were still slowly being released. So there was a huge cardboard case displaying the red and blue albums standing on an end cap. It stood about five feet tall and was filled with CDs. I picked one up, glanced at it, put it back, and then turned around. Then I approached the rope where Kate Bush sat less than ten feet away from me. I was on her left side and watched as she signed some stuff and talked to people. She was drinking from a tall Poland Spring bottle which she placed down next to a small container of Tropicana orange juice. There were a few other people next to me. One guy called out "Kate, we love you," and she turned around and smiled in our direction. Then the security guard came.

"You guys can't be standing here. Gotta move."

Another guy asked her to marry him. She acknowledged that with a laugh and glanced back at us again.

"Come on guys, let's go," security said, motioning us out of the way. I went back toward the Blue Album display and picked up a CD again. I wanted to say something to her just to know I had made some kind of personal connection with her, but there wasn't much to say. The only thing I would have said to her had I waited in line was that she should tour. Not even ask her if she was going to tour...just tell her that she needed to tour. There was a demand for it, and she had an audience out there who wanted to see her. She was legendary...*oh for fuck's sake, she knows this!* What was I going to say? I knew I wasn't going to use the word "tour" on her, because I was sure she had heard it all the time and was answering that question with every fan that approached her since she arrived in the city. Where in New York City could she play if she did in fact tour? I wondered. The Garden? Nah...she's not that big. Roseland? Nah. She'd fill it up, but she's too classy for a place where most of the audience can't sit down. The Beacon? A decent size place for her, and she'd probably have to do multiple nights. I didn't stick with the Beacon Theater though. Radio City Music Hall was what popped into my head and stuck out. I turned around and approached the rope.

"Buddy, I'm not gonna ask you again. I said you can't stand here. Ya gotta move."

I ignored him.

"Kate..." I said with the security guy placing his hand on my shoulder. "Kate, Radio City is waiting for you," I blurted out. She turned around, smiled at me and waved. Once that happened, I didn't even notice the security guy anymore, but at some point just after that, he grabbed me by the arm and pushed me.

"Let's go!" he shouted as I stumbled back, trying to regain my balance to no avail as I knocked into the Blue Album display, sending it to topple over onto the floor with me landing on top of it. Laying in a pile of CDs and cardboard, it wasn't until two security guys were picking me up off the floor that I realized what had happened.

"Are you alright?" the guy who pushed me asked. "I asked you nicely to move and you didn't move."

"You need to chill out dude," I said to him, spoken from my 23-year old punkass mouth as the two guards escorted me down the aisle where I headed out the door without their assistance.

"I was only saying hi."

"Yeah, well you should stand in line like everyone else. You think you're special?"

I stepped out onto the sidewalk, turning around just outside the opened door.

"Yeah motherfucker, I *AM* special! I'm Mike Fuckin' Derrico, and one day you'll be guarding *MY* fuckin' line!"

I still don't do lines.

7

THE DEADHEADS, THE DEAD, AND THE DEAD

Deadheads have always scratched their heads over me, wondering what to make of me. I love the Grateful Dead, but I was never a Deadhead. I've never followed them on tour, never collected tapes of live shows, and never walked around outside the Shoreline Amphitheater holding one finger up in hopes of a miracle ticket. Sure, I've seen them live a handful of times and own every album, but I've invested no more significance in them as I have in most of the other obvious and usual suspects of classic rock. Oh, how I cringe when I use that term willingly...classic rock...but the very fact of my using it is testament to the inevitable passage of time, classification of periods for historical purposes, and the idea that rock as we once knew it has in fact passed us. More to my smaller point though, I never gave the Dead any special treatment over bands like...say...Led Zeppelin, the Who or Pink Floyd. I think of them as just another band in that crucial chain of important Boomer-era bands. Of course, there are many bands that I prefer over the Dead hands down. But generally, I don't like or dislike them any more than most acts lying around the classic rock gene pool. With this in mind, the fact that I've always been surrounded by Deadheads for most of my life is worthy of mention and exploration within these pages. That means that out of the common courtesy and good will of many of these people, I was always given many tapes of all the important shows and kept in the loop. And even though I never had the urge to send away for enough mail order tickets for an entire tour, I still maintained enough interest when my friend Mark would call me from places like Atlanta or Albany at three in the morning to tell me the setlist. Even though I didn't walk the walk of a Deadhead, I was informed, educated and familiar enough to talk the talk with the best of them.

Deadheads are funny in that they've never really cared for the studio albums. It was always about collecting and trading tapes of the shows. I guess that's the one thing I always found unsettling about the Deadheads...their disinterest and indifference to the Grateful Dead catalog. Always driven by the live show and the spontaneity of the moment, they never had any use for the studio albums. Of course, like anything else there are exceptions. However, for the most part, I've found it next to impossible to discuss the studio albums with my Deadhead friends. For instance, I can have someone sit in front of me and recite the setlists for the entire spring 77 tour, yet if I ask what their favorite song is from *Wake of the Flood*, they'll say something like "What songs were on that one?" or "the studio albums suck."

The world of the Grateful Dead was an island unto itself. It was a large and glorious island unlike any other entity in the history of modern music. But it was so self-contained, that the fanbase rarely strayed too far from the family tree. They listened almost exclusively to the Dead and Dead-related bands and artists. I always think of the line *when you stand too close to something, you can't really see it.* It perfectly describes the conditions under which many Deadheads have been unable to view the Grateful Dead within the context of the rest of the rock world. It is difficult to observe something from the outside world and asses its place in the outside world when you are very much on the inside, and rarely, if ever, leave. So for someone like me, the studio albums have served as vital maps of the band's evolution as well as markers of the band's treasures. Sure, you can't find gems like "Wharf Rat," "Birdsong," "Cassidy," "The Eleven," and "Turn on Your Love Light" in the form of Dead studio recordings (not counting solo albums), thus dividing the two impressions of the Dead on the rest of the world. There is the Grateful Dead as a vital part of the rock and roll world with a worthy respectable catalog of classic albums and music...and there is the Grateful Dead as center of its *own* world, yielding an entire secondary catalog for the hardcore obsessed. So with that, it is quite possible to watch the band improvise their way through fifteen songs over the course of two sets and an encore, and only have a third of those songs come from studio albums. This is one of the unique elements of the Dead. A large percentage of their most-beloved live tunes are not even featured on official studio releases, something almost unheard of within the rest of the rock world. It is difficult to imagine Kiss fans being pleased after having gone through an entire Kiss concert that featured maybe only four songs from actual Kiss albums. Same goes for Rolling Stones fans that are comprised of the ones who go for the hits, and the ones who go for the chance of the occasional rare album cuts...point is, those fans know the albums well. A Stones fan might come out of a concert saying, "Damn, they didn't play anything from *Exile* tonight!" To the contrary, you would never hear a Dead fan coming out of a show saying "Damn, they didn't play anything from *Go To Heaven*!" It's just not the way the Deadhead mindset operates in relation to the setlist. It is purely about the moment and following it wherever it leads over the course of any given night...the same spontaneity that I'd later get from Patti Smith shows. And while the Deadhead experience has been purely physical and spiritual (I remain envious of the people who had the conviction and fearlessness to live that life) they'll never quite know the intellectual masturbatory joy of pitting Side One of *Blues For Allah* against Side Two of *Terrapin Station*, and then analyzing and dissecting the artistic components that such a discussion would entail. In all honesty, I'd much rather be able to just experience the music and fill my downtime with something else such as football or videogames. Sometimes I think I'm cursed having to live a life where I spend just as much time *thinking* about music as I do *listening* to music. But then I consider the nature of my personality and how I'm just as insular in my own mind as the Deadheads are on their own musical island. Music is an intellectual experience as well as a physical and spiritual one. Anyone who might disagree with this sentiment is not paying attention, not thinking at all, or is probably just an asshole.

While in the middle of my Italian film phase of 1993, I took one particular afternoon to head over to the Angelika where some new movie, *Especially On Sunday* was playing. The movie was released and flopped rather quickly, and I don't remember a damn thing about it, nor does anybody else. It was Monday, September 20, and I was in the city for a Grateful Dead show during one of their early-Nineties residencies at the Garden. After the film, I met Tom, Mark, and our friend, Dave over at Hunan Pan for dinner. Following a quick bite, we walked out on Hudson Street as the sun began to go down just after 7PM. It was the last night of summer and still fairly warm. We all got into a cab and headed north as Hudson turned into Eighth Avenue until we got out at Thirty-First Street and ran into the building at the Southwest entrance. The show itself had some standout tracks like "Baba O'Riley" and "Tomorrow Never Knows," but I wasn't particularly thrilled with the setlist, although I was glad to get "Dire Wolf." I think that fourth of six shows stands out in Dead history as the night Edie Brickell showed up to guest on "Space."

I associate that particular change of seasons as the start of an underlying eeriness and just overall sense of something bad in the stars that seemed to hover over the next few years. Even though it was still a relatively remarkable time for music (and the arts in general for that matter), there was an undercurrent of fatalism snaking its way through the mid section of the decade...one that would short circuit the sense of community still alive within the rock world. Late in October, a massive retrospective celebrating the career of Italian director Federico Fellini opened at the Film Forum on Houston Street in the Village. *Tutto Fellini* was a monstrous six-week marathon that would see every single Fellini film shown in glorious restored print and would run through early December. On Halloween, I went into the city with my friend from work, Jorge. Jorge was a Seventh Day Adventist who was always wrestling with his faith and searching for answers and meaning in life and death. Jorge knew me as the long-haired crazy lunatic freak at work, but he seemed to be amused by my intellect and shared intolerance for common mainstream culture. He had a strange respect for the fact that I preferred tofu to meat, PBS to CBS, indie films to Hollywood, the New York Times to the Star Ledger, cafes to bars, reading to sports, and museums to clubs. Whenever he needed a "day of culture," he'd hang out with me. Jorge wasn't by any means hip. He was borderline-square, and experienced true culture shock as the streets became packed and closed-in with freaks from all walks of life converging on the Halloween Parade that would be starting at 7PM. We had tickets for the 7:30 showing of Fellini's *La Strada*, and decided to grab some low grade Chinese food at the King's Express on West Eighth Street. It was one of those brightly-lit takeout places with jade green walls that always had at least two or three tables in the back. As we ate, I gave Jorge a brief history of Fellini, his films, his influence and why we were so lucky to be going into the city to see one of his celebrated works on the big screen. This was no ordinary film, I told him. You couldn't just go see this at the multiplex in New Jersey. He asked me if Fellini was still alive and making movies. I told him the filmmaker was in his early eighties, not very active anymore, but was just honored at the Oscars with a Lifetime Achievement Award earlier in the year. Jorge seemed to be looking forward to seeing *La Strada*. I gave him a background of the film and informed him that the actress Giulietta Masina who stars opposite Anthony Quinn was actually married to Fellini in real life and the two had been a longtime couple. Giulietta became the staple face to a handful of Fellini's early works and she had indeed cast an indelible mark on Italian cinema. After Jorge finished eating, he wanted to buy a t-shirt he'd seen at the Postermat across the street. I was still working on my shrimp in lobster sauce, so to save time he got up and went over to the Postermat while I finished eating. As I sat there alone, I reached for the headphones of my Sony Walkman and put them on. I pressed play, and suddenly the cassette inside was playing me a live 1971 Dead show from the Fillmore East. I finished eating, sat back, stretched my legs out, folded my arms and closed my eyes. It was one of those moments where all was right with the world...those rare moments where you realize you're content with everything around you and there was no place else you'd rather be. I listened to what had become my favorite version of "Easy Wind" and let the song play out until Jorge came back. He sat down and I took the headphones off. He showed me some shirt that read New York City on it and I politely responded with a "cool" or something. The radio in King's Express which was tuned to one of those Hot-something stations that played Bon Jovi and Michael Bolton-style hits had gone unnoticed during the duration of our time inside the establishment. When the news came on, it quickly grabbed our attention and without warning, transported us into a world of the surreal. First, they announced that the young Hollywood star, River Phoenix had died at the age of 23. Jorge and I looked at each other. *Holy shit*, the collective look on our faces said. We were both 23 as well, and it was the first time anyone our own age who had gotten famous had died. Was this going to be our generation's James Dean? Just as I was swallowing the news of River Phoenix, the next sentence to come out of the radio was that legendary Italian director Federico Fellini had also died. Needless to say, I was in shock at this news, especially under the circumstances in which I heard it. Jorge couldn't believe it either. One minute I'm telling him all about Fellini while we're about to go to a Fellini film festival, and the next minute we're told that the guy just died. We sat there stunned for a few minutes, but then got up without missing a beat, pressing on toward the exit to once again hit the street where we'd trudge through the Halloween Parade across Sixth Avenue and hit the Film Forum. Walking out, the Grateful Dead's "Touch of Gray" began playing as we stepped into the chill of the crisp mid-autumn air.

Shortly before twelve on the night of Wednesday, March 23, 1994, my friends Tom, Dave and Mark were heading back from Uniondale, Long Island where they'd just seen the Grateful Dead at the Nassau Coliseum. It was the first of a five-night run before the three of them would embark on an excursion down the East Coast to follow the remainder of the spring tour before it would wrap up in Miami within a few weeks. It was Tom who was driving and just getting back onto the Belt Parkway while Dave and Mark talked about the next night's driving arrangements. Locked into the moment just as they had been all night, all three of them looked up and out the window where something caught their eyes from the distant and seemingly unreachable line on the horizon where they first saw the explosion followed seamlessly by the mushroom cloud. And then the sky lit up orange and red.

Shortly after twelve on the night of Wednesday, March 23, 1994, now the morning of March 24, I was at Eric's house flipping channels on the TV. I was feeling under the weather and probably should have been home sleeping. The past few nights had been late ones, having gone to the David Letterman show on Monday where Tori Amos was the musical guest. She came out and did "Cornflake Girl" from her new album *Under the Pink*. The following night, a few of us went up to the Meadowlands racetrack to watch horseracing. I really should have been in bed as I sat there contemplating the chills running throughout my body. Inside the other room was Eric, his girlfriend Agnes, and two of our friends, Jay and Al. Going through the high-numbered channels of the cable spectrum, I stopped at CNN where Giulietta Masina was pictured in the top left corner of the screen. The Italian actress and wife of Federico Fellini had died at the age of 73, less than five months after her husband. The door opened and Agnes came out. She walked across the room and sat down on the couch next to me.

"Dude, put the Rangers rewind on," she demanded, taking the control out of my hand, changing the channel to MSG. The nightly ritual was to drink and watch a replay of the Rangers game that usually occurred earlier in the evening. Within another minute or two, the guys would be coming in and hockey would fill the room deep into the AM hours. I wasn't a fan, but I would always root for New York no matter what the sport. The Rangers were hot that year, and talk of the Stanley Cup was a constant. This was going to be their year.

Who gives a fuck...I'm going home.

As I got up, I was almost knocked back down on the couch by a powerful force of warm air that moved through me and shook the blinds on the window. Agnes felt it too.

"Dude, what the hell was that?" she whispered, looking at me wide-eyed.

Inside, the glass sliding doors were rattling. We could hear Eric begin to freak.

"Holy shit, man! What the fuck is *that*?!"

"Holy crap!" Al followed.

"What the fuck is *that*?!" Eric railed again.

Frozen in place, I was almost afraid to go into the bedroom where Eric, Al and Jay were looking out the glass doors. Behind the doors was darkness...the backyard, a fence and the Oak Woods beyond the fence. The woods extended south at least half a mile, but what lay beyond them was in no way visible from Eric's windows. From the backyards onward, it was just solid woods.

Again...

"What the fuck is *that*?!"

Eric was pointing outside toward the woods.

And then I saw it.

Somewhere, possibly inside the woods...or maybe beyond the woods...so huge that it gave us the distorted perception that it was closer than it really was...was a fireball...a wall of flames moving and swaying violently like a King Kong-sized bonfire fire between the distant trees. We couldn't make out what it was, nor could we be sure exactly *where* it was. I opened the sliding door and we could immediately hear a roar in the distance. It was a blowing sound so intense and overpowering that the only way to describe it is to imagine the sound a 300-foot blowtorch would make. What was even more unsettling was the amount of light outside. In the midnight hour, there was daylight over the entire development and farthest reaches surrounding. It was a broad and eerie daylight, engulfed and enveloped in an ominous reddish orange that made up the entire sky.

"Are we fuckin' nuked man?" Al screamed in nervous laughter.

"Dude," Jay shot back. "If we were nuked, we'd be dead."

Eric offered the next possibility.

"Holy shit...did a plane crash or something?"

I thought the same thing.

"Yeah, that's gotta be a plane that went down in the woods."

"That's not in the woods bro," Eric replied. "That's too far away to be in the woods!"

"Yeah," I agreed. "You're right!"

It really was hard to tell where in the hell this giant wall of fire was, but as we all gathered out in front of the house anyone on the block who was awake had wandered outside into the street. Many were running down the block toward the main highway to get a clearer perspective on where exactly the fire was coming from. Rather than stand outside in the street speculating with the neighbors, we all got into Agnes's car and drove toward Route 1 where once we got there, the entire fireball, much like a mushroom cloud rose high above the skyline of Central Jersey like an orange and red monster that could swallow entire towns. When we got on Route 1 South, it looked as though maybe the Menlo Park Mall was on fire or perhaps even exploded given the massive size of the hovering flames. But then we rode past the mall and all of it was intact, empty and without activity. We could see the fire, but the more we drove, it didn't seem like we were getting any closer. That's just how big this thing was. You could keep going toward it thinking it was maybe a thousand feet away, but you never got there. Kind of like having mountains on the horizon. Eventually, we stopped at Metuchen Train Station. Agnes parked, and Eric, Al and Jay got out, running up to the track where they could get a better view of the massive wall of flames in the sky. I stayed in the backseat, not wanting to get out and see it enough to etch it permanently into my mind's eye. It wasn't something I wanted an indelible vision of. I was also feeling feverish and really just wanted to go back. Agnes searched the radio for reports of anything. I told her to put on CBS-AM which was a 24-hour news station, and sure enough they were talking about a gas explosion in Edison, New Jersey. It turned out to be a long night for anyone who was awake in Central Jersey, and if you lived anywhere in the tri-state area, chances are you could see the fire from many miles away. Eric, Al and Jay came down from the train platform after about ten minutes and got back in the car. We went back to Eric's by 1 AM. Shortly after arriving back, Tom and Mark came by after dropping off Dave. We all sat on the floor in Eric's ground-level bedroom. We could see the fire through the trees just past his backyard. And we could hear the gas-fueled roar of the flames. I tried to take my mind off what was going on outside by asking the guys about the show. Mark happily read off the setlist:

First Set: *Shakedown Street, Little Red Rooster, Row Jimmy, El Paso, Might as Well, Promised Land*

Second Set: *China Cat Sunflower, I Know You Rider, Women Are Smarter, So Many Roads, Truckin', Drums, Space, I Need a Miracle, Standing on the Moon, Good Lovin'*

Encore: *U.S. Blues*

The Grateful Dead were in Miami when Kurt Cobain's lifeless body was found in Seattle. On April 8, 1994, the spring tour was wrapping up and our friends were about to head back up the East Coast. Back at home, a handful of us sat around quietly that Friday night, trying to make sense of what had happened. A month earlier, Cobain had OD'd in Rome. Early in those reports, there were already rumors he had died. Something like this seemed inevitable, which is why I really wasn't surprised when I heard the news about his death late that afternoon. The immediate sense around the music world that seemed irrefutable was that something significant had happened, and a devastating blow had been dealt to the future of rock. It was not one of those things that occur in retrospect where critics and fans realize something important had happened and it constituted a full-fledged rock revolution. It was not one of those things you realize *after the fact*. We *knew* something big was happening all though 1992. 1993 saw grunge and alternative established as a full-scale rock movement within the mainstream of popular culture. By 1994, we were right on the cusp of watching the earliest evolutions take place within this new kingdom of artists. Eddie Vedder got a chance to evolve. Cobain, not so much. 1994 began with the momentum of '93 still in full swing. It ended with the tumultuous release of Pearl Jam's *Vitalogy* amidst the defiance of a reluctant Vedder who was supposed to carry the torch. Or so they said. He just didn't agree. Plus, he was busy locked in a silly battle with Ticketmaster at the time. If only he could have picked his fight with the company in 2014 as opposed to 1994. Who knew that after such bad publicity in the Nineties, 20 years later, Ticketmaster would be so out of control and corrupt, redirecting logged-in members on their site to a scalper's site where customers were charged well over face value? Who knew that while scalping agencies were buying up lots and lots of tickets in the Nineties, that Ticketmaster would get in on the action a few decades later? And who knew that while Vedder was expected to carry the burden of whatever had been up Cobain's ass, Pearl Jam had already created their best music by 1994 and rock would fizzle out into parody, mediocrity and eventual invisibility on the same mainstream scale?

So what happened?

Well, it sure wasn't Vedder's fault, nor was it Pearl Jam's. Vedder came down to earth and learned to navigate his success and stardom in a measured and responsible way, surrounding himself with the right people...many of his own influences as opposed to his peers... and allowing his maturation to be reflected in his art. He'd associate with Neil Young, Bruce Springsteen and R.E.M. He'd become politically active, immersing himself in social justice causes. He'd still rock, but he'd cross over into a world of adult concerns like so many of the best and most respectable artists did. And Pearl Jam would continue to turn out uninteresting music while still managing to sell out arenas in every major city for multiple nights. They'd become classic rock, part of the establishment, and Vedder, like his heroes, would become one of rock's elder statesmen. They'd be revered and respected just on their name alone.

But rock in the post-Cobain Nineties wasn't just about Pearl Jam. Radiohead, another of the alternative era's most promising bands would turn out one of the great masterpieces of the decade, and then do a complete 180, striking their music out of shape and becoming the anti-rock band, all but eliminating guitars from their sound until they had their cliché *return-to-form* moment years after anybody gave a shit and they were already too old to be revolutionary anymore. Stone Temple Pilots, a band that had some catchy songs, but couldn't shake the Pearl Jam-wanna-be comparisons had already bottomed out while their singer made junkies fashionable again for assholes. Smashing

Pumpkins quickly became irrelevant before decade's end. Soundgarden was on the outs and so was Alice In Chains. By 1997, Lilith Fair was as "fuck you" as rock could possibly get, but the "fuck you" wasn't a *revolutionary-movement-against-the-establishment* "fuck you." It was more of a male-bashing sorority that saw a rise of women with acoustic guitars writing feisty "we'll show em" songs, and standing in fist-pumping solidarity. *Good for them*, I thought. Some of my favorite artists were always women, and I eventually started to hate the categorization of male and female in the industry and the way artists were referred to. Chuck Berry and Bob Dylan were never referred to as great male artists, but when someone like Jewel Kilcher appeared, it was always *Oh, here's a great female artist!* Patti Smith has always been my favorite, though on some days I'd put Suzanne Vega above everyone. Anyway, by the mid-to late Nineties, a great chunk of the music scene, at least in America, had become all about Jewel, Sarah McLachlan, Meredith Brooks, Tori Amos, Fiona Apple and Paula Cole. Scraping the end of the century, it was a great culmination for the latest wave of feminism (though not quite Riot grrrl), and a beautiful thing for self-empowerment. Ani DiFranco was the most independent of all of them because she operated outside the confines of the music industry and took far more risks artistically than the mainstream artists who gathered around Lilith Fair during those years. Personally, I could never dig her music because it quite honestly made me nervous. There was something about the way she played her guitar that made it sound like a squirrel was running up the neck and it gave me anxiety. Unfortunately, with the exception of Rage Against the Machine, these artists were as close as the late Nineties got anywhere near something ballsy across countless miles of pop rock music. The only thing that resembled actual rock by way of the mainstream was catchy and syrupy watered-down versions of whatever Nirvana and Pearl Jam did first...bands like Bush, Matchbox 20 and Limp Bizkit, one of many acts suffering terminal confusion over what they wanted to be and who they wanted to appeal to. Rock was well on its way to a place where the idea of crossing over into other genres was no longer the exception, but the rule. Still, there was an audience for it and it thrived for a while. With that, the second half of the Nineties barely resembled the first half. And while that is true for most decades of the rock era, the last few years of the twentieth century progressing into the new millennium saw rock having its testicles hacked off by paper cut, one slice at a time. Acts like Kid Rock represented a new era where artists had a foot and a half in rap, and half a foot in color-by-numbers rock. He seemed confused in those years when he did everything he could to convince you he was a rap star, and then he tried a few years later to pass himself off as a rock artist...hence the hybrid and the first generation raised on both. The only thing that seemed clear was that the era of originality in rock was over. Every important rock song had been written, and now the next generation of rock artists was about to dabble in a little rock, a little rap, a little country, a little of this and a little of that, and it was all going to be friendly and safe. The real hip hop artists were the ones who would be the actual groundbreakers in the new century. Regarding appearances, rock, for the very first time in its history would no longer inform the fashion trends, but would begin to follow them.

And so, while many younger kids for whom grunge was the first and only rock to be exposed to, the changes by decade's end were appealing. The sight of grown men in backwards baseball caps, no shirts, and baggy shorts, jumping around the stage while grabbing their testicles was far less rock and roll than anything we'd ever seen. To be fair though, the silly stylistic antics were not just exclusive to Limp Bizkit and Kid Rock. It's difficult to pinpoint where exactly the murder of rock fashion began, but it's precisely one of the major things that had always turned me off of some of the era's older bands like Red Hot Chili Peppers. Though I have always loved Flea as an artist and a human, I was always repulsed by those bands that literally bounced around the stage half naked, lumbering like cavemen.

So what is my point?

My point is that by the late Nineties, the *cool* had drastically fallen out of rock music. It became corny and clumsy in both sound and vision. Regarding the bands that stayed within the rock framework, even they lacked the element of cool. Rock stars with character were suddenly endangered, as no-named, nondescript front men of the new generation all looked more like models in an Abercrombie and Fitch catalog. Even popular bands like Blink-182 looked as if they were fitted in the wardrobe department on the set of *Beverly Hills 90210* for the episode where Brenda and Dylan get tickets for that rad punk concert at After Hours. And for any wiseass who feels compelled to mock my *90210* analogy, be warned...I was a closet viewer right up until the end, and no such episode exists. But that's just how uncool and sing-songy rock had become. More on *90210* later.

Cobain's death did not kill the future of rock music. It killed the present. It cut short the moment. It was a moment that while held up in hindsight to hypothetical scrutiny, might have lived up to whatever the myths suggest it could have been, or could simply just have evolved into something else. Instead, it just became nothing more than a moment in time. The question of the legacy of Nirvana, Pearl Jam and grunge itself becomes more significant as time goes on, however. What *was* that legacy? How influential were they *really*? Where are the generations of guitarists that Kurt Cobain was supposed to have influenced? If in the 30-plus years since grunge, all we had to show for it was Nickelback, Bush and Creed, the true influence of that entire era needs serious re-evaluation.

The wind went out of the sails completely some sixteen months after the death of Kurt Cobain when Jerry Garcia passed away in his sleep. They say he died with a smile on his face. I don't know that to be true, but I like to believe it. It just works symbolically on so many levels. Jerry's words about taking the whole trip a step ahead or even a few steps ahead was as eloquently put as anything involving the counterculture and the push toward a more progressive civilization. On the night of the day Jerry died, I was at a Santana concert. It was August 9, 1995. Carlos Santana came out and told the crowd that he was playing for us with a heavy heart. The feeling was mutual all the way around the venue. Garcia was the first major blow to rock's second generation since Lennon 15 years earlier. It was a muggy summer night, beautiful otherwise. But aside from that feeling of doom that seemed to still be pervading how our lives were affected in relation to the music, the 1990s had turned a corner. But it wasn't just the Nineties. It was the beginning of feeling a stamp of permanence. Of finality. In the space of just a year and a half, the symbolic future of rock had been exterminated, while the emblematic past had begun to expire.

8

NEW PARTY (THE BIRTHDAY SHOWS)

They say you should never meet your idols. The big reason usually given for this is that it's extremely difficult to digest when you realize how fragile and human they really are in the face of the deified perfect-to-your-image mold that you've boxed them into. Another reason is they might turn out to be dicks, and that might be hard for you to accept...especially after having that image you've held so long be shattered in front of your face. Luckily, that's never happened to me.

There was only one time I went all fanboy on someone. For the most part, I've avoided almost every celebrity/artist I've stumbled upon in the streets. In New York City, it's customary to not acknowledge the famous, unless you happen to be some star-struck tourist or outsider or something. As a suburbanite from New Jersey, I've always adhered to the New York City custom, not because like the city, I was too cool to address the famous, but because I really didn't care. There was nobody on the planet whose autograph I wanted. Nobody I wanted to stand in front of and tell how fucking great they were. People were people.

Sure, there existed the artists that I elevated to a position much higher than the realm of reality in which I grouped everyone else, but it was their *work* that afforded them such a place of reverence and regard. Take Bob Dylan for example. He's Shakespeare to the entire era of modern pop music. He's the center of the entire canon. But why would I want to meet him? To shake his hand? To tell him something he's heard infinitely each day from assholes like me approaching him while he's trying to eat dinner? I've tried to imagine meeting Dylan, and every time I have, I've struggled to come up with something to say to him because I honestly have nothing to say to him. Maybe thanks? But even thanks is a little far-fetched. Thanks for what? Making me see the superficiality in people and things I thought to be real? Making me realize how cool I still needed to be? Making me unable to turn a blind eye to the dark side of human nature? Making me a humanist?

In essence, fucking me up irreversibly?

Gee, thanks Bob.

On the second anniversary of Jerry Garcia's passing, I ran into Patti Smith on MacDougal Street. It had been a day of coincidences. Earlier in the morning of that August Saturday in 1997, I stopped at Lucca's Café in downtown Metuchen, New Jersey to deliver a handpicked Patti Smith mix tape to a girl named Kim who worked there. Kim, who always served me my coffee before my trips into the city, was a kid fresh out of high school about to start at the New School in the Village that fall. This girl had all the physical trimmings and trappings of mid-late Nineties college students...the septum piercing, tattoos, and a head full of white girl locks. She also had a mushroom obsession and was always talking about the work of Terence McKenna, trying to get me to read his books. One day, she gave me a copy of *Trialogues at the Edge of the West*. In return, I gave her a mix tape in an attempt to turn her onto Patti Smith's music. Kim had only heard of her and knew of her. Patti was important, and someone like Kim had to at least be introduced to the world of Patti's work.

"Awww," she said smiling, "there's a song called Kimberly!"

Then she chucked the tape aside and took the next customer's order.

My usual Saturday thing was to have lunch at Hunan Pan, see a foreign or independent film that I couldn't see in Jersey, and then head uptown to the Metropolitan Museum of Art where I'd hang out through sundown and into the evening hours. On this particular occasion though, I had my cousin Paul with me. Paul wanted to spend the afternoon rummaging through some record stores, so we stayed in the Village all day. Late in the afternoon, I was going through bootlegs in Revolver Records. In the days before downloading and Youtube, bootlegged shows, like everything else, were bought hard copy. Bands like the Dead allowed taper sections in their shows, so they of course are among the few exceptions. Most of my boots were purchased on cassettes, either from flea markets, conventions or writing a guy named Al Odum whose ad we found in the back of magazines. Al was primarily a name associated with Kiss bootlegs. In the event that I wanted a show on vinyl, I'd go to Revolver. Inside the store, Paul wandered over to me as I was pulling out a recording of a 1978 Patti Smith show from Philadelphia, a bootleg titled *To the Ones She Loves*. I glanced at the cover, amused. It was a show I had on cassette, but this was the first time I was seeing the vinyl.

"Who are they?" Paul asked, pointing to a photo of Patti with two older people, a woman and a man. The woman had a cigarette literally dangling out of her mouth. They were Patti's parents.

"Those are her parents," I told him. "This is awesome," I said, "look at that. This is so rock and roll."

An hour later, we were walking out of Café Borgia on the Northeast corner of Bleecker and MacDougal. We started walking south toward Houston, and stopped at the corner next to a woman and a little girl who caused me to do a double take. It was Patti and her daughter Jesse. The four of us just stood there waiting at the light. Jesse, maybe around ten at the time, was holding some shopping bags and Patti was eating a sandwich of some sort, possibly a gyro, which happened to be breaking apart with the entire contents falling out of the bread and into the street. Grease was running down her arm as she held it up to wipe it off. This could have potentially been an embarrassing situation for her, but she didn't seem to give a shit. This was all happening as I was saying hi and doing the shitty fanboy thing, proclaiming what a huge influence she had been on me and all the rest of the nauseating bullshit that she didn't want to hear at that particular moment in her life.

"Well Mike," she said casually and totally in stride. "I hope I haven't influenced your table manners."

Chunks of meat continued falling onto Houston Street as the sandwich was barely in one piece anymore.

I noticed we were dressed almost exactly the same in navy blue t-shirts and blue jeans. I quickly told her how it was becoming a day of coincidences, having given a personally-chosen mix tape to a girl named Kim who was taken aback that Patti had written a song called "Kimberly," and then running in to her an hour after rummaging through her bootlegged shows. I left out the part about the bootlegs, of course. As I spoke, Patti was fixated on a button I was wearing that was pinned to my shirt. It was the word *Fuck* written as the Coca Cola logo, and she leaned in toward me to see what it said. Then she became distracted and turned toward the street. Jackson Smith, her 17-year old son was crossing from the island in the middle of Houston Street and coming toward the corner where we stood. Patti introduced me to him and then to Jesse. Jesse just stood by and smiled politely as if she were used to this sort of thing...strangers like me approaching their mom as they were trying to live their lives. I told Jackson that I was at both Irving Plaza shows a year earlier when Patti brought him up to play "Smoke on the Water." He smiled and nodded in recognition of the shows.

"Well, we have a new album coming out next month," Patti said, giving me some totally unexpected news that made me feel I was perhaps the first person outside her own camp to hear about it.

"Really? Very cool. Is it new music?"

"All new songs," she confirmed.

Sure enough, a few weeks later, the album *Peace and Noise*, a title given to her by Jesse, was announced with a release date of September 30.

And what a day September 30 turned out to be that year. It was a day in which Bob Dylan, the Rolling Stones and Patti Smith all released new albums. There was no real indication yet by the end of 1997 that anything was all that different in rock music. The key players, old and new were still involved, and quite a few were still firing on all cylinders. Sure, it was a year where teeny-bop pop came back with a vengeance and laid the course for how the turn of the century would unfold. So while acts like Hanson and the Spice Girls were everywhere that year, we still got acclaimed new albums from Paul McCartney, Bob Dylan and Patti Smith. Dylan's *Time Out of Mind* even won the Grammy for Album of the Year. Radiohead, one of the few grunge-era bands to outlive the Nineties and transcend the decades released *OK Computer* and gave us one of the more ground-breaking works of its time. Nineties acts such as Stereolab and Spiritualized were also peaking creatively, though not anywhere close enough to the mainstream rock world to make a cultural dent. What was a wall of creativity and influence just five years earlier had become spotty at best, and this was still pretty difficult to notice given the fact that rock was still largely recognized. But all of that would change within a year or two. Hip hop would become prominent, universally respected and ultimately dominant in the pop world following the success of *The Miseducation of Lauryn Hill*, the 1998 Grammy Awards *Album of the Year* by ex-Fugee member, Lauryn Hill. The album did not by any means serve as the main catalyst for the hip hop takeover. The long-term influence of hip hop and its place within pop culture had already been well-established by then, though the album certainly boosted the genre up with some much-needed credibility on the mainstream stage for the naysayers. I guess I was one of them, but the Lauryn Hill album blew me away as did her follow-up *Unplugged 2.0* several years later. My knowledge of hip hop has always been below 101. I could never develop an ear or a taste for the Gangsta stuff and always preferred with absolute reverence the New York rap of the Eighties...Grandmaster Flash and the Furious Five, Afrika Bambaataa, Kurtis Blow and the sonic political collage of Public Enemy. This all fits in beautifully with my lifelong obsession with 1970s and 1980s New York City subcultures.

Boy bands like Backstreet Boys and NSYNC also oversaw the invasion of the pop charts as we got closer to the millennium, and bands like Matchbox 20 and Goo Goo Dolls appealed to the saccharine crowd while clown acts like Kid Rock and Sugar Ray were picking up right where Vanilla Ice left off a decade earlier. They seemed to be proud of what they were doing too...as if this were the natural progression rock was supposed to take. I don't doubt the sincerity or conviction in these artists toward the music they were making, and I'm not knocking their art. I'm sure they all believed in what they were doing and each of them was far more successful than I ever was as a musician. It's just that none of it was cool and none of it did anything for the good of rock music as a whole. With all of this happening simultaneously, one would think that I would have been completely disillusioned with the entire scene, but I was so consumed by the veteran classic artists during those years that it would take a considerable amount of time to realize how bad the drought really was. During those years I became pre-occupied by Bruce Springsteen's reunion tour with the E Street Band and the fact that Bob Dylan was turning out masterpieces (Time Out of Mind, Love and Theft) again. It was Patti Smith though, who more than anyone, got me through the late 1990s and early years of the new century.

Going back to that glorious transitional year of 1989 when at the age of 19, I was discovering Patti's music for the first time, it really does seem another lifetime. Outside of growing up with "Because the Night" on the radio along with the brief airplay of "Frederick" at the initial release of the fourth album *Wave*, I hadn't fully experienced the Patti Smith Group in real time. I knew nothing of the Beat Poetic Symbolist Existential Punk Apocalypse entailed in their music until I randomly picked up their second album. In short, *Radio Ethiopia* blew my mind, knocked me off any musical course I thought I knew to be real and concrete, re-shuffled the deck of my conscience, and literally changed my world. The underlying tragedy for me of course, was that Patti had retired from being a rock star in 1979, got married to Fred Sonic Smith of MC5 fame and retreated to the Motor City where they raised two kids and lived a normal life. Well that was great for her, but it meant that I would never get to see her perform live, nor would we ever get new music. I say "never" because these things seemed written in stone at the time. Granted, she did put out a "comeback" album in 1988, but it only amounted to a one-off tease. The songs also hinted at domestic bliss, and the fire and fury of her original run of albums was missing. Still, *Dream of Life* was a masterpiece as much as her earlier albums *Horses, Radio Ethiopia, Easter* and *Wave* were. But it was a different kind of masterpiece...one from an adult and parent's perspective with a watchful eye on the state of the world and the future, and a refreshing sense of optimism. Released during an election year, *Dream of Life* was the right album at the right time.

On July 8, 1993, I got what I initially thought to be a once-in-a-lifetime chance to see Patti when it was announced that she would make a one-time appearance at Central Park's Summer Stage. In the midst of a heat wave where temperatures soared to 100 several times that week, Patti took the stage to an overwhelming response from an enthusiastic crowd that was there to let her know she was sorely missed. She read poetry and did not perform any music. Still, we took what we could get and loved every minute of it. Near the end of the night, Patti took questions from the crowd. As the customary one-person-at-a-time Q&A began, questions were thrown at her from all over the audience. And from the height of the grunge era, the inevitable *What do you think of Nirvana/Do you like Pearl Jam* questions ricocheted all over the outdoor venue to no response. The closest she came to acknowledging such questions was when a girl asked her, "What do you like to listen to?"

And there it was.

Silence.

We anxiously awaited the response.

"What do I like to listen to?" Patti said, echoing the question and pondering for a moment.

More silence in the hot, sticky but clear New York City night. And then her angelic voice echoing through the P.A. speakers over the crowd, soaring well throughout the immediate surrounding vicinity within the park, and breaking the silence.

"I like to listen to the laughter of my children."

Long story short, it was through multiple tragedies that Patti Smith re-emerged after Fred Sonic Smith passed away on November 4, 1994 at the age of 45, followed just a few weeks later by the untimely passing of

Patti's brother Todd. In one of the more emotionally-draining nights of music I've ever experienced, and a bittersweet one at that, Patti returned to Central Park Summer Stage in late July of 1995. This time she brought Lenny Kaye, her longtime musical partner since 1971 and guitarist for the old Patti Smith Group.

Patti Smith's audience is an empathic bunch, made up of humanists...intellectuals who thrive on music, art, literature and cinema... progressively liberal for the most part...rock and rollers who understand that rare connection between the punks and the Beats that's embodied in her work. Punks who can tear up a room through the raw energy of the moment...and gentle sympathetic souls with a conscience. The Central Park air was heavy with the knowledge of Patti's recent irreplaceable losses, but the crowd was with her through every second and every step during moments when she periodically broke down between lines of new songs like "Farewell Reel," a heartbreakingly uplifting nod to Fred with the reassurance that she and the children would go on, rise and flourish. Between "Farewell Reel" and "Paths that Cross," it doesn't take much for me to break down myself when I think back on that beautiful night.

By the end of 1995, Patti was back out on the road through the coaxing of Michael Stipe and Bob Dylan. She did a brief tour with Dylan in December, recollecting Lenny Kaye and Jay Dee Daugherty from the old band and recruiting younger musicians Tony Shanahan and Oliver Ray as crucial contributors to her newly-formed band. One of the more surreal moments of my concert-going life was seeing Patti and Bob Dylan standing face to face at the same mic singing "Dark Eyes" together. It's always cool to see your favorite artists live in concert. It's dreamlike and bizarre when you see them performing together.

On the eve of the millennium, my friend Michael Ziggy of the band Turn Me On Dead Man and I went to Patti's birthday show at the Bowery Ballroom. The Bowery Ballroom was a new venue on the Lower East Side that opened in 1998, and Patti's year-end shows became an annual event for the next 14 years. Historically speaking, that's not a lot of time. But for a while, it seemed that it would all go on forever, and that no matter what was going on in our lives during any given year, that year would end with Patti's birthday show followed the next night by her New Years' Eve show. Patti is often associated with CBGBs and with good reason, given her indelible history with the club in its most legendary era. However, the venue I most associate her with is the Bowery Ballroom. Much more than CBGB could ever be, the Bowery Ballroom became a kind of home base for Patti concerts. If CBs represented a glorious decadent, albeit brief flash of time, the Bowery seemed fit for the long haul, as Patti, Lenny, Jay Dee and Tony, all well into adulthood, offered shows speckled with a relentless and certain continuation of the chaotic beauty of their past legacy...now marked by the wisdom of balance, a fellowship of benevolence, the magical creation and mangled humor of spontaneity and the combustibility of the moment it all encompassed.

The December 30 birthday show became a staple in my year-end activities for a decade and a half. The birthday show served as a summation. As fans, we too were pretty well into adulthood during those years, but not too old where we were totally fucking jaded yet. We were still young, we were going to change the world, and we always left with a sense of hope. Even if it wasn't the world...even if it was just our own individual lives, where we walked out of that show feeling as if everything was going to be alright, whatever it was. I'd walk out feeling as if this was going to be the year I got my shit together. This was going to be the year I was able to fucking exhale for once after years of feeling the walls close in a little tighter. Nobody did empowerment like Patti Smith.

As the final 24 hours of the twentieth century began to wind down, Ziggy and I entered the Bowery for what was billed as the Millennium Concerts. Upon arrival we were handed complimentary CDs made specifically for the December 30 and 31 shows that read *Patti Smith and Her Band, The Millennium Concerts.* Underneath, it read *New Party.*

As the turn-of-the-century approached, I was 29 years old and living a pretty existential existence working for a pasta and olive oil company. The company was always good to me, but the working environment was far too hostile and abrasive. I was down in the dungeon of taxing physical labor...the warehouse and an adjoining area known as the Oil Room. This was where olive oil was packed in an assembly line set-up surrounded by 1500, 3000 and 6000-gallon tanks holding various blended versions of product. Trailing intersecting pipes carrying oil from tanks criss-crossed over our heads with half a dozen pumps running together in roaring unison at ear-splitting volumes. The doot-doot-dooting of forklifts in permanent backwards motion provided additional constant sound on top of the multi-pump canvas. The conditions were not favorable to my fragile 131-pound frame, which wasn't cut out for physical work...lifting and tossing 55-gallon drums five high onto an empty 80-foot trailer with broken rotted floorboards. One time I was driving a forklift onto the trailer and began to fall through the bottom. Weather conditions made you feel like you were outside even though you were inside. No heat in the winter, no air conditioning in summer, no windows to see daylight. Winters in the drum trailers were cold but summers were deadly when 90 degrees outside meant 130 degrees inside. Life had become unsettling and unacceptable. This was not the way it was supposed to be years earlier when I had my entire life ahead of me. What I wanted was to get out of that life and go back to school. I'd be turning 30, and all I could think about was how all my friends seemed to be happy and having fun. Many had started teaching careers and always had their summers and holidays off. I remember going to work on Martin Luther King Day and one of my friends being appalled that the company was open. Upstairs in the office where everyone was white, it was business as usual, while the black people downstairs in the dungeon had to take a personal day if they wanted the day off. I remember thinking, *this is fucked up. I need to get back in school.* Most of the guys down there were straight out of prison and most were recovering heroin addicts and alcoholics. Upon release from prison, they'd often go to halfway houses which required them to sign up with a local temporary employment agency, which would send us temps every week. Everyone's story was the same when we first saw them on Mondays. They were all broke, and the ones who would get in your face would be hitting you up for money. They'd stay two weeks and get paid. Then they'd relapse on heroin and we'd never see them again. Then the new ones would come the following Monday and the circle would go around again. But again, the company was good to me, and I had plenty of benefits and paid time off. They always got pissed off though when I would save my last three vacation days for the last three days of the year to do Patti Smith's year-end Stone Pony/Bowery Ballroom shows. And so, going into that particular birthday show on December 30, 1999, I was feeling extra anxious and extra hopeful for something...some kind of sign... some sort of life-changing inspiration. At some point between songs, almost reading my mind, some girl cried out "Patti, I hate my job." Patti, facing the drums with her back toward the audience, turned around in the direction of the girl, perhaps seeking her out with her eyes to find where in the crowd she was. Then she approached the mic with the most serious of concerned expressions.

"Quit."

A few months into the new century, Patti and the band threw a release party at the Bowery for the forthcoming album, *Gung Ho*. I remember this night, February 16, 2000 for two reasons...meeting Clive Davis and being part of a video shoot for the song "Glitter in their Eyes." The band played their usual nearly-2-hour concert and then asked the audience to stick around. The shoot lasted close to an additional hour as "Glitter" was played through the PA and the band pretended to play it while Patti lip-synched and the crowd went nuts as if it were all still a concert. The filming moved through about three takes of "Glitter" while Patti called some rarities in between. Two songs in particular that I'd never witnessed live before or since..."Seven Ways of Going" and "Revenge"...two treasures from 1979's *Wave* album were priceless to hear. While I was always hoping for "Elegie" and never got it, these moments reinforced the spontaneity in the event and the feeling that anything can happen. "Elegie" was a song I liked probably more than anything on the *Horses* album. Situated at the tail end of Patti's classic debut, "Elegie" served as a meditation on death and a remembrance of those we've lost over the years. It carries the weight that comes along with the desperation of helplessly missing someone who is no longer there, and the irreparable void that could never be filled in someone's absence. Patti, who has soldiered on in the face of losing so many of her loved ones along the way, wrote the song in her early twenties when everyone was still very much alive, youthful and exuberant. Through her own youth, Patti precociously wrote with the wisdom of a sage...praising and mourning the artists...those who have impacted her life and work...Arthur Rimbaud, Paul Verlaine, Jimi Hendrix, William Blake...ghosts of the past that have adorned her writing and music. She's walked among these ghosts throughout her adult life... or more accurately, they've walked beside her. She's always felt their presence...taking the most vital components of their own artistic existences, and for those closest to her, their best personal attributes that continue to influence and guide her through life. They come to her as they come to most of us... in the wind...in dreams...in the flight of a bird...in the smell of a cup of coffee or the sound of a hundred-year old aria. They serve as little messengers that inform the dark through the light. The last lines of "Elegie" highlight what is perhaps the darkest, most haunting ending to a rock album that's ever been recorded...as Patti drifts through memories...the past rising to the surface, reflecting on the loss of artists and friends who make up the canon that all our inspiration has drawn from, quoting two Hendrix songs..."1983" (A Merman I Should Turn to Be ...) and "Are You Experienced"...citing the trumpets and violins that she can hear in the distance...her skin emitting a ray though the lament that our friends can no longer be with us on the physical plain.

"Elegie" was a song that always haunted me in a good way. It's important to note that this was long before Patti and the band started playing the *Horses* album in its entirety, so in those early days of her return to performing in the late Nineties, (what I call the second phase of her musical career) I always wished she would play "Elegie," and she never did...at least not while I was there.

9

HOW THE GUITAR BECAME UNCOOL

I will need to quote myself in this next passage. "Think about Jimi burning his guitar...the whole sacramental thing onstage at Monterey. Guitars became like a weapon. It was a fucking machine gun. It was an extension of your cock. The iconic visuals of rock and roll...it was the most powerful image and symbol of rock music. But not anymore."

What happened?

One of the more profound answers to that is never considered and I've only heard myself speculate on it in my own show, the *Rock Under Fire* podcast. But in order to get into that, we need to remember another instrument for a few seconds, the piano. If we think of guys like Little Richard, Jerry Lee Lewis and Fats Domino, and imagine them banging away on the piano as they often did while their songs were becoming early staples to the rock canon, we then must consider that the piano was once a primary instrument of rock and roll music. The guitar wasn't yet the all-powerful object it became toward the late Sixties into the Seventies. But at some point as that decade turned over and rock journalism and photography began to create the myths and images that would accompany the narrative, the piano began to lose its power and respectability...at least to the critics of the Hipper-Than-Thou School. While the guitar became essential due largely to the band structure of guitar, bass and drums, and the inevitable phenomenon of guitar gods like Hendrix, Clapton, Beck and Page, pianos became associated with artists like Liberace, Barry Manilow, Elton John, Billy Joel, the Carpenters, Captain and Tennille, etc... Billy Joel, one of my favorite artists, once said something to the effect that the hipper-than-thou critics would have taken him more seriously and assigned him more rock credibility if he had played a guitar instead of a piano. Put into a nutshell, the piano simply became uncool during the 1970s, when 15 years earlier, Little Richard and Jerry Lee Lewis made it sound like it came straight from the crotch. Regarding the magnitude of Elton John during that decade, he was just as much a visual freak as anyone in 1975, fully equip with the complete rock and roll lifestyle of total debauchery. Yet, he's never been put into the same sentences as the usual critics' darlings or revered cult figures. In other words, if "Benny and the Jets" had been written by Lou Reed or Mark Bolan, or performed by David Bowie instead of Elton John, it would be regarded as a glam classic, perhaps a masterpiece, and not just another hit single for Seventies hits collections. What I am suggesting is if Elton had strutted the stage with a mic stand instead of standing at a piano, the visual would have lent itself to his image, and his image would have changed how he was perceived within the larger picture of the rock world.

Fast forward a few decades into the twenty-first century where rock is virtually invisible in the big picture. Let's put that aside for now while assessing exactly *who* is playing the guitar in the new millennium. We know that the rock bands that do exist still use them, but we can take the biggest rock bands of the past 20 years, and most of us would be hard-pressed to name the guitarist of any of those bands. We won't find them on posters in Spencer's stores and we certainly won't find them on the bedroom walls of middle and high school kids. Those kids aren't playing The Black Keys. They're playing video games and hearing classic rock songs from the Sixties, Seventies and Eighties filtered through video game and movie soundtracks, and they don't know the artists, so it all sounds like traditional music ala "Happy Birthday," where nobody can account for who made the song. Unless of course, they have a father or grandfather who may tell them, "Yes, son, that's Led Zeppelin. Kids your age used to worship them and every 14-year old boy wanted to play an electric guitar and be Jimmy Page."

One alarming fact of the 2010s was that electric guitar sales were down drastically. If kids were picking up a guitar at all, it was most likely an acoustic. Electric guitars became a combination of "artifact of the past" and an object of competition ala Guitar Hero/Rock Band, where the guitars in video games were closer to guns that rack up points than they were to musical instruments that you actually learned to play. The rare occasion of teenagers who could play something as intricate as "Eruption" or shred on some 1980s-style wankery, was treated as something phenomenal as if it hadn't been seen before. It became common on social media sites to see Youtube videos posted of the exceptional teen or pre-teen who can wail like Eddie Van Halen.

Whoah, check out this kid from Japan!

12-year old Shocks Classmates with Finger Taps!

Kid Shreds on the Guitar!

It makes me wonder...had Youtube existed in 1986, the videos of kids playing "Eruption" would far exceed the videos of the rare kid playing "Eruption" today, because *every* kid played "Eruption" back then. Of course I'm exaggerating, but you get where I'm coming from.

Guitars, for the most part, had two uses in mainstream culture during the 2010s. The first was as a piece of kitsch. They were ironic props in much the same way as old-school rock t-shirts on non-rock artists at award shows. Justin Bieber posed with one at an awards performance early in the decade. Madonna has used one onstage since 2001 to strum a D chord every once in a while. The second was the legitimate use of the guitar as an instrument, but the majority of songs containing guitars featured acoustic guitars, which served merely as inconsequential objects that accompanied syrupy ballads by whiny sensitive males. This musical format is nothing new and harkens back to those piano 1970s when that guy Dan Hill was writing songs about wanting to hold you 'til he dies. But now, this template for what constitutes mainstream guitar pop has become the rule and not the exception. Dan Hill singing about wanting to hold you 'til he dies existed at a time when there were lots and lots of rock artists dominating the mainstream and co-existing with other genres on the charts. There was no shortage of rock music that was consumed and listened to in large numbers. But what does it say for rock's presence as a pop cultural entity in the 2020s when every mainstream rock artist is Dan Hill, and every song is about wanting to hold you til he dies? It is no accident that Ed Sheeran was as popular as he was during the 2010s and rock stars went from larger-than-life chic to the non-descript style of nameless males in fashion ads. Sometimes I think the Ray character from *Beverly Hills 90210* was inadvertently the prototype for this brand of artist. But Ray never made it all that big in music because he was coming up in a music world that still had actual rock stars, and people still knew the difference between what was real and what was not. Or to sum it up, people still gave a shit that it was music for people who don't really give a shit about music. This is what writers like Kelefa Sanneh would dismiss as a *rockist* attitude that rock fans tend to have toward those who are okay with plastic mediocrity. But getting into that inevitably leads us into the question of "artistry," and the unsupported poptimist conviction that half-a-century of songwriters writing and performing their own songs that have survived as classics making up much of the bedrock of modern pop culture is not artistically more relevant than the current trend of performers having three to 21 songwriters and three to six producers to stitch together a three-and-a-half minute pop song. But that's jumping off the page because we're talking rock, not pop, and it's moving our attention away from our focus on the guitar, so we won't go there.

So, really. What happened to the guitar in the twenty-first century? Like the piano in the 1970s, it became uncool. Seriously...what would Lester Bangs say? As someone who seemingly despised rock stars, would he praise this period of stagnation? Or would he finally have learned to appreciate what we had?

10

THINGS LESTER BANGS GOT WRONG (OR DID HE?)

Among all the documentation of rock history that has been recorded over the years, there is one piece that reflects the trends and changes better than anything else preserved. I've always felt a spring 1980 Lester Bangs interview with Sue Matthews serves as a marker and perhaps the best measure of where rock had been at the halfway point, how far it had come, and where it was expected to go...at least according to Lester Bangs.

Why Lester Bangs?

Why, among the dozens and dozens of other critics who penned the history of rock and roll as we know it, does Lester Bangs deserve this distinction in my book? Plain and simply because he is one of the very few who could be trusted. He wasn't in the business of making rock stars look good in exchange for acceptance into the establishment...which means he was free to be honest. And let's face it...he's turned out to be the most accurate.

As we recently entered the fifth decade since Lester Bangs left the planet, I often find myself assessing the things he either foresaw, hoped for or was just plain right about concerning the future of rock and roll. And then some things, he just got wrong...not because he was wrong... but because the things he merely hinted at, actually played themselves out to extents that he couldn't have even imagined. It's also tempting to visualize how Lester would have reacted to the things he missed that proved to be culturally relevant like the advent of MTV and the imperative nature of music videos that suddenly became an art form in addition to a promotional medium. Lester, who didn't like the star system in rock and didn't think it should exist outside of Hollywood, may have been delighted at the disappearance of the rock star during the twenty-first century when Dave Grohl became the lone token rock artist for the masses. That said, he would have had a blast with guys like Bono and Axl Rose and events like Live Aid and *We Are the World*. Still, even in the desolate 2020s, rock stars remain plentiful...saying farewell or dropping dead one at a time...while the ones who don't say farewell and/or drop dead are ridiculed for sticking around. Yes, that is to suggest the sad truth...that nearly every major rock star on the planet in the 2020s is over the age of 50. With the Rolling Stones being the template and litmus test for what's possible, they're also one of the few acts old enough to have made it past the ridicule stage and have been commonly and universally accepted as some geriatric entity that rocks rather than a bunch of aging rock stars still in the process of *getting* old. They're no longer aging. The Stones have existed as an old band for far longer than they existed as a young band. Most living generations except for the Boomers remember them *only* as an old band...and so now, at least in 2023, they're treated more as lovable teddy bears who rock fans no longer take for granted...much more than they're thought of as the bad boys and societal threats they supposedly were more than half a century ago.

Lester Bangs never saw the Rolling Stones as a model for some cultural revolution as they were often portrayed to the mainstream in the late 1960s. "Street Fighting Man" fooled no one who knew any better. The business model the band would thrive on for over half a century was already in place, and by the late Seventies, in their early thirties, they were already some of the biggest pigs that ever existed, according to Bangs. Long before the astronomical absurdities of Ticketmaster's corrupt dynamic pricing, Lester was calling out the steep $12.50 that it cost to see Ron Wood and Keith Richards as the New Barbarians at Madison Square Garden...two and a half dollars above the average ticket price for major acts in 1979. The stigma of being a rock star in your thirties was heavy baggage by the late 1970s, and many artists just didn't know how to act or evolve or even stay in the picture. Pete Townshend struggled particularly with this unprecedented situation in rock music and by the end of the decade, was second guessing his very existence as an artist. It would contribute largely to his decision to put an end to the Who with a farewell tour as they entered the 1980s. *Imagine staying in the game and playing rock and roll music in our forties!* And so, acts like the Stones would begin a phase of their careers that took up the majority of their history...as an old band. The Stones as an old band on borrowed time didn't begin with 1989's *Steel Wheels*, as some may believe. They were already being scorned for sticking around too long as early as 1972's *Exile on Main Street*. But the Stones weren't self-conscious about their role the way Townshend was. And if ever a band didn't give a shit, it was the Stones. And maybe there was nothing more *fuck you* than old people playing rock and roll. Lester foresaw this and declared that the Stones should continue making albums and playing into their sixties or perhaps until they drop dead onstage.

There is no overstating the idea that rock music was initially an experiment. It was made by the young, for the young, and our rock stars were not supposed to get old. There is also no overstating how very old these guys *already* seemed when they were in their thirties. Timeline is everything. Modern pop culture begins in the 1950s with the teenager, television and rock and roll. There was no precedence for rock artists aging. So, when Lester suggested the Stones should play until they were old and decrepit, the idea seemed far-fetched with the future so far off and so remote, that we would never get that far anyway. Little did Lester know that the Stones would be playing well into their seventies...more than 40 years after he made such a comment.

Older rockers like Townshend insisting it was time to pass the torch to a younger generation that barely exhibited anything new, original or remotely exciting to begin with seemed pathetic to Lester Bangs. If artists in their forties could pull it off and do it, they *should*. And that's what I cover in my earlier chapter *The Real 1989*, when this generation of artists finally came to terms with their forties, and then, pushing their fifties, initiated the unforeseen second acts of their careers. As newer and younger rock acts would become less and less relevant to pop culture over the next three or four decades, this generation of artists in their fifties and upward, would remain the biggest concert draws well into the twenty-first century. Something Lester could hardly have anticipated when he passed away in 1982. As the Millennial and Z generations steered toward hip hop, country, video games, and disposable pop, Baby Boomer artists were still driving the market for rock concerts with a built-in nostalgia culture being the only element keeping rock music visible on a mainstream scale. This is usually where the neo-hipster argument comes in..."But rock is just as relevant today, if not bigger. There are so many bands out there...you just have to know where to look for th..."

Yeah, we'll take that one apart a little further ahead.

Regarding the dinosaurs, Lester was one of the few people who already saw and acknowledged a nostalgia culture informing trends. Or maybe not informing them, but directing audiences to circle back to past trends. What Lester referred to was the manner in which the 1950s, during the 1970s, were revisited and portrayed in a very reverent sentimentality. TV shows such as *Happy Days*, *Laverne and Shirley*... films like *American Graffiti* and *Grease* and music acts like Sha Na Na. What Lester didn't get to see was the emerging pattern of popularity that every decade of modern pop culture would assume in 20-year cycles. By the end of the Eighties, the Sixties, particularly the counterculture would become fashionable again by way of the holy dollar, and in a much more profound manner than he had first suggested. It was Lester after all who predicted that the 1960s counterculture would eventually be absorbed into American capitalism. Another generation of kids otherwise raised on heavy metal discovered the Grateful Dead, Jimi Hendrix, the Doors and Bob Dylan. The peace symbol became more a fashion statement than what it represented 20 years earlier. Tie dyes were plentiful, as were candles and incense sold in suburban shopping malls all over America...spiritually themed stores such as Journey and East Meets West that catered to rock music in the t-shirts they sold and to the Eastern mysticism that accompanied the hippie mindset way back to the 1960s...hence the meditation focus devices...mandala tapestries, tapes and CDs filled with sitar, rain forests, thunder storms and mountain streams. Buddhas, Shivas and Bhodisatvas occupying shelves next to beaded necklaces and shawls made of hemp and burlap....after the sum total of the Eastern trip bleeding into the flaky new-age culture, thus allowing for all the Enya CDs that occupied the end caps by the mid-1990s. Even the massive outdoor three-day Pepsi Festival of 1994 got fronted as Woodstock 94 under the guise of a celebration of the original Woodstock's twenty fifth anniversary, but this time capitalism was unapologetically front and center, not reflecting or representing anything of the liberal hippie values of the first festival.

By the late Nineties, the Seventies finally reclaimed its place in the hearts and imaginations of popular culture. Films like *Saturday Night Fever* had come upon their twentieth anniversaries and the Bee Gees were suddenly adored again...even taken seriously by all the rock-centric minds that once sneered at them the first time around. It takes 20 years for pop culture to come full circle. Some ten years after something was initially popular, it often passes through a backlash of rejection...in some cases an embarrassing cringe factor is associated with it in a "What were we thinking" mockery. In 1988, ten years after they owned the pop charts, the Bee Gees could not have been more unpopular and uncool. In 1998, the Baby Boomer and even Generation X had gained enough distance from it all to learn to appreciate, miss and even love not just the Bee Gees, but much of the disco music of the Seventies.

By the turn of the century, nostalgia culture was in full effect. MTV, a once-influential channel playing music videos had long ceased to be a music channel at all, with a more adult/contemporary version of MTV called VH1 suddenly changing its format into a more youth-friendly channel, catering to Millennial acts like All American Rejects, Avril Lavigne and tunes about Stacy's Mom, 1985, and the car being in the front yard...with nearly every popular song featuring the same whiny, sing-songy vocal style that Blink-182 is almost single-handedly responsible for. When it became evident that rock was no longer a vital force of any kind in mainstream youth culture, the music format was stripped at VH1 as well. Once hip hop became the center of the universe, it coincided with the early stages of downloading, streaming and Youtube, so technology dictated that video channels like MTV and VH1 were no longer needed for promotion and exposure. Instead, VH1 catered to the first two generations of modern pop culture...the Baby Boomers and Generation X, with shows like *I Love the 70s* and *I Love the 80s*. It no longer had a hand in reflecting or informing the times, so it didn't even try.

For those offended, it's not that there were no Millennial or Gen Z rock artists...it's just that none of them have made a real cultural impact remotely close to the rock music of the twentieth century. The majority of the rock market circa 2023 is driven by Baby Boomers and Gen X looking backwards in the form of Broadway musicals, obligatory box sets and twenty-fifth anniversary editions of groundbreaking or culturally relevant albums, revival package tours in sheds and theaters, biopics, etc...Lester Bangs scratched the surface. Nostalgia culture wasn't just a trend in the 1960s and 1970s as he seemed to think. It informed the next nearly-half-century...and as long as people over 40 continue to lament the loss of the good ole days, it will never go away. If Lester Bangs only knew.

11

ROCK UNDER FIRE

As rock lay on life support during the first decade of the new millennium, I hadn't thought all that much of the state it was in. I hadn't yet arrived at any conclusions, probably because I was busy ignoring everything happening in the industry, and the fact that there was less and less rock music of substance at the forefront of pop culture. And I'm not even comfortable with that last sentence because it suggests that rock had *anything* to do with pop culture during the early 2000s, when it had *nothing* to do with it. However, I'll leave that sentence in there, and go along with the suggestion that it was *less and less* at the forefront as opposed to *invisible*. I'll leave it in there for the whiners who like to tell themselves that rock is as big as ever in present time (2023).

It is perfectly okay to accept that not everyone lives in a historically significant era...that major movements and revolutions don't happen in the arts for every single generation. Yet, the neo-hipsters, especially millennial neo-hipsters would have us believe that we are living in anything but a dormant period. If anything, the first few decades of the twenty-first century will most likely be remembered as a transitional period where the Internet came into full realization, and pagers became cell phones and cell phones became smart phones. Yet, as cutting edge as we may think we've been, we're merely in the same stage of Internet and smart phone technology as airplane technology was at the time of the Wright Brothers. When we consider the first few decades of the twentieth century, we often think of an overlap where the nineteenth century is still very much present in certain areas. Then at some point, whether through technological advances...things like medicine, automobiles and airplanes, or the social progress of the progressive movement...the twentieth century *became* the twentieth century. When historians look back on the first few decades of the present century however, it is quite possible that the only thing they will associate with it in terms of historical significance (politics aside) will be technology. It is also likely that nothing of note will be marked in the realm of art and music, much less rock music.

It very often gets speculated upon. Who in rock music will be remembered 100 years from now? Let's consider two styles of music outside of rock. Let's consider classical and jazz for a moment. Out of several centuries of the broad scope of what is generally known as classical, albeit Baroque, Romantic or what have you, there are only a small handful of people that remain household names and whose music is still available in your local Barnes & Noble music section. These names include Mozart, Beethoven, Bach, Vivaldi, Wagner, Stravinsky, Verdi, Puccini, and a few others. I'm even tempted to suggest that the immediate memory of collective mainstream conscience would only recognize Mozart, Beethoven and Bach...the big three and that everything else is either secondary or simply falls away from the surface of immediate thought. That's to suggest that other outside elements more modern to the subject have in recent times brought names like Verdi and Puccini to the mainstream, namely Luciano Pavarotti, Placido Domingo, Jose Carreras, and later on, Andrea Bocelli whose performances of Verdi and Puccini arias became household melodies during the modern pop era. That is not to suggest these names and works weren't popular pre-modern times, but they were no doubt brought successfully into pop culture as *we've* known them. Outside of these certain modern influences, it is tough to imagine operas like *La Traviata*, *Rigoletto*, *La Boheme* or *Tosca* being as on-hand to suburbanites without some bankable artist to pull them into modern times. So, with that, and respect to the major works of say, Rossini and Wagner, we still have only a handful of names that are as commercially accessible on the surface a few hundred years later.

Let us now consider jazz. What happens when we draw our second non-rock example from the same century in which rock existed? Jazz has quite a number of decades on rock and roll, but both were thriving by the late 1950s, rock in its infancy and jazz possibly at its peak. It was a long illustrious century for jazz, and the names just as in any other style of music, were plentiful and impossible to contain. Yet, the surface of mainstream awareness only allows for textbook names such as Louie Armstrong, Duke Ellington, Count Basie, Charlie Parker, Dizzy Gillespie, Miles Davis, Charles Mingus, Thelonious Monk, Ornette Coleman, John Coltrane, Erroll Garner, etc... I carefully use the *etc* rather than a concluding *and Errol Garner,* so as not to suggest my inferior and inefficient 101 knowledge of jazz doesn't boldly declare these names as the only artists in the canon. Though it is safe to say that the number of jazz artists that *most* people immediately think of is roughly the same number of classical artists, give or take a few. What is startling however, is that the classical names go back several centuries while the jazz names go back only a few decades prior to (and sometimes blending in with) modern times.

If most of the artists who represented the bulk of jazz music presented during the middle decades of the twentieth century are forgotten about within 50-60 years, how can we rationally expect many names to be remembered of the early years of the twenty-first century 100 years later? Especially given the fact that nothing...*yes, nothing* significant happened in rock music since the early 1990s. The bottom line is that when nothing creatively influential, artistically valuable or culturally significant happens during any given period of time, nobody will remember most artists 10-20 years later, let alone 100. This kind of hypothetical speculation is pointless, however, and believe it or not, I spent an entire episode of the *Rock Under Fire* podcast talking about it.

In April 2016, I began what initially started as an experiment with two friends to see if we could pull off our own podcast at a time when podcasts were really beginning to peak and it was becoming apparent that anyone can do one. It would be three guys talking about rock music.

How fucking original.

First kiss of death, as there were thousands of other podcasts talking about rock music. If we could get up to ten episodes, we'd be lucky. So when we got up to around Episode 20, we settled in for the long haul. The idea of the show was to talk mostly about the place of rock music within the twenty-first century and how it's become virtually imperceptible if not totally invisible compared to everything else driving modern pop culture. There's that word again. In fact, words and phrases I repeat unapologetically in these pages...invisible, zeitgeist, pop culture, big picture, mainstream...may at times make you the reader wishing I had grabbed a thesaurus more often. But I shit you not...these are the correct words to use in such discussions. Repetition drives the point home.

Rock Under Fire was a relatively unknown podcast with a modestly small but loyal audience. From 2016 to 2023 through six seasons, we turned out shows every two weeks for six months out of the year. Eventually, the consistency of my co-hosts became less and less over time and I ended up doing solo shows through much of the final two seasons. Thankfully, I had some great guests in those last 30 or so episodes who helped me take the podcast closest to what I initially envisioned when it began. I was never comfortable with the formality of introducing the show at the beginning of each episode...or plugging websites and social media...or introducing people. I wanted instead, total spontaneity. Eventually, shows were beginning in mid-discussion whether the audience knew what was going on or not. I rarely introduced guests anymore unless it was somebody famous. I wanted the listener to feel as if he or she walked into a room in the middle of a really great conversation on music but was limited to the fly-on-the-wall experience. But at some point during the Covid shutdowns, I began having discussions away from rock and roll. It was really the only way I could deal with the staleness of having boxed myself into a corner by limiting the podcast to music. I did a few book reviews and had some authors on plugging their books, including my own. One episode was spent talking about some protests going on in Cuba at the time. Another one was about a sports card business my co-host Pat had started. Anything that got us away from having to talk about Van Halen for the hundred-billionth time. I remember talking to author

Gina Yates for over three hours one night about her book *Narcissus Nobody*, and we ended up getting into a marathon discussion about love and relationships. Fuck it, I thought...this is going to be the episode whether it's about music or not. It was then that I realized two things. One, it was the best episode I ever did for the *Rock Under Fire* podcast (with the lone exception of my interview with Alice Echols about disco)...and two, I no longer wanted to be constrained by the subject of music. It was then that I decided to put one final season into motion rather than just abandon the whole thing completely. We did have some great musical episodes during that shutdown year (Season 4), but as the concert industry began reopening after the shutdowns, Pat and I began discussing things like masks and vaccines. Shortly afterward, I began getting negative feedback over why we "went political." Even during the final season, an old high school friend outside a local tavern told me he loved the show until we started "getting political." When Pat and I were talking masks and vaccines on the show, we were addressing as a *music podcast* the things that were crucial, decisive and pertinent to the state of the concert industry at the time of closing in 2020 and eventual reopening in 2021. That was discussion based on how the *music industry* had been affected by Covid, and although I didn't see it as "political," I knew this type of mentality...and anything short of total agreement with Donald Trump and conspiracy theories was considered "politics." So in response to the comment, I did what I always did and changed the subject after a halfhearted chuckle... tempted to tell that person, "we've always been political."

A few days after ending the podcast, I was sitting at my desk editing the final episode. Outside my window, one of the neighbors was in his driveway washing his car with music playing in the background. He's an outside guy who is always gardening and doing some sort of work around the exterior of his house while rock music cranks in the garage from one of those satellite radio channels that play mostly Seventies. Distracted and unable to work, I sat back becoming entranced by Paul Simon's "American Tune." It's a song I've heard my whole life...a song I know inside out. One of the artists/acts we never talked about much on the podcasts is Paul Simon/Simon and Garfunkel, but Paul is easily a Top 10 songwriter if you ask me. I might even put him in my Top 5. So I sat there listening...and in some ways, it hit me as if I were hearing this familiar song for the first time. I shut the window to muffle the outside sound and went to my streaming app, pulling the song up under Paul Simon. Listening a little more privately, I realized that the song seemed to be an opposite bookend or perhaps a 1974 update of the 1968 Simon and Garfunkel hit, "America." That song, "America," always made me think of the tagline of the 1969 film *Easy Rider*.

Two drifters went off to look for America but they couldn't find it anywhere.

The idea is consistent. Two people walking off to look for America. It was a common theme in the 1950s and 1960s. Jack Kerouac wrote his acclaimed *On the Road* dealing with the drifter, the Beat poet, the questioning youth...disillusioned with the promise of his country, aimlessly traveling the highways of America, *in search* of America. What that meant exactly is never really explained by anyone. Not in *Easy Rider*... not in Kerouac...not in Simon...and not in any truly complete way in most rock and roll songs. Many have come close in asking those questions, and some have even tried to answer them. But what is at the core of what people search for? Tourists go to Washington. They visit the Capital...the Pentagon...the White House. They go so they can maybe get some sense of the power of the government. Or perhaps the symbolism or the myth. Or maybe even feel some sort of vibe rooted in this *idea* of something called America. America is a nation of immigrants because of its idea...this living myth known as the American Dream, which lures so many, but only comes true for so few. It brings people from all over the world in hopes of a better life. "American Tune," uses imagery of American symbolism to evoke a questioning sentiment of his country. He talks of arriving on the Mayflower...the ship that sailed the moon, and of "the age's most uncertain hour." The image of the Mayflower, a time when those first Europeans were inhabiting the so-called New World all the way to the age's most uncertain hour, which could be the uncertainty of arriving in a new country and starting over, the common story of America itself...or it could be the uncertainty of the America in which the song was written...a country torn apart by Vietnam, Richard Nixon and Watergate.

It was always apparent to me that Paul Simon loves his country but more so the idea of his country. It's all over his work...the pure Americana of "Mrs. Robinson" and "The Dangling Conversation." The unrest of "The Boxer" and "America." There is a pessimism and a questioning that often threads its way through his work, but the deep love of America's roots is there. I sat there thinking about these things. It occurred to me then and there that while "Sounds of Silence" may have been Simon's most successful song, "American Tune" may well be his most important contribution to American poetry. While "Sounds of Silence" is preserved by a naive idealism, "American Tune" is marked by a mature and withered witness to something that has clearly not gone right. The singer wonders what's gone wrong. In first person, he surveys his country and asks what's happened. Does he even recognize it? In a dream, his soul rises above his body as he's dying, offering him a smile of reassurance. Then suddenly, he's flying...and out in the distance he sees the Statue of Liberty drifting out of New York Harbor. For many people, the Statue of Liberty, perhaps America's greatest and most well-known symbol, was the first thing they saw while approaching from the Atlantic. It represents the promise of American freedom. While those of us born here often take it for granted, it must have been a profoundly powerful sight for those seeking something better. Yet, from America's beginnings, there has always existed the element of class warfare, racism and a widening gap of haves and have-nots. Simon's vision of the Statue floating away is no doubt consistent with a dying dream. The protagonist of the song only raises these thoughts and questions, however. He is not caught up in them. Maybe he's suggesting that all of those ideals of the 1960s hardened people in the 1970s when the counterculture seemingly collapsed. This was long before the left won the culture war when all that existed in the States in relation to *right vs. left* was disillusion. They were going to change the world. As David Crosby said, they were right about the war and they were right about drugs. They were right about peace and love. So, what happened? Did they get complacent in their American lives? Did reality suck them in as they joined the "real world?" Or as the morose and one-dimensional conservative mind suggests, did they simply *grow up*? Simon's protagonist looks around, questioning and tossing out thoughts, but in the end shrugs it off. His main concern and perhaps only real concern doesn't go past his own backyard. He has bills to pay and a job to do. Maybe a family to feed. Tomorrow is another working day and his only concern is the immediate...getting some rest. He is only an observer if not just another spoke in the wheel. Yet, he presses on with tomorrow because it's the only thing he can do.

"American Tune," though probably not Simon's best song is a careful reflection of what became of the American Dream, if it ever in fact existed. He wrote it in the early 1970s, following the counterculture's demise when the consensus was that nothing about America was going to change for the better after all. The counterculture would be vindicated and validated time and time again over the course of the next four decades as the country would grow more liberal and tolerant with a progression toward that promise of liberty and justice for all...but in 1974, the collective disillusion within America, regardless of which side you were on, was real. If one searches the writings of the major poets of that generation, the sentiment of the early 1970s was essentially the same. What began a decade earlier with the questions of Dylan's "Blowing in the Wind" and the warning that the "Times They are a-Changin," ended with the Who screaming "meet the new boss, the same as the old boss."

I sat there thinking about all the times I talked ad nauseam about how rock was once the center of mainstream music and reflected the state of the world through social, environmental and political injustice causes, and how it informed pop culture in every possible way. I thought about how an artist can write a song like "What's Goin' On," "Ohio," "Power to the People," "Imagine," "Redemption Song," "The Message," "Fight the Power," "Rockin' in the Free World," "Sunday Bloody Sunday," "Revolution," "U.S. Blues," and there would be a collective acceptance of it within the world of popular music and into the fabric of social justice activism, which was hand-in-hand for more than half a century all the way back to Woody Guthrie. I thought about the political right in today's divided climate under FOX Americana... and how if any of these songs were written today, it would probably be calling for boycotts and the cancelation of artists like Bob Dylan and Paul Simon and Neil Young and Bob Marley and Edwin Star and just about every major artist in the history of modern popular music. I started thinking about how I'm actually ashamed of my generation... this generation that calls itself X and prides itself on drinking water from a garden hose. It's my generation...the children of the hippies... that somehow through some tragic karmic twist of fate ended up becoming the crotchety uptight generation of "shut up and sing."

I can remember in the Eighties when Tipper Gore joined up with a bunch of Republican senators wives to form the Parents Music Resource Center, a group that fought to put warning labels on music that contained profanity, sex or violence in the lyrics as a means to alerting parents to the content before purchasing said music for their kids... or just to let parents know what their kids were listening to, which in hindsight doesn't seem all that unreasonable. To make their point in Washington, they targeted a handful of artists as examples of their concern. Tipper Gore's involvement with the PMRC however, overshadowed the group itself for the simple fact that she was the wife of a Democratic senator and a liberal who was aligning herself with Republicans. But rock and roll, from day one, has always been a liberal cause. Conservatives have been railing against rock music for the better part of seven decades. From the moment Elvis Presley appeared, racists down south got offended because he was a white kid playing black music, and so there was a collective effort to smash Elvis records and ban him. Then they went after the Beatles for John Lennon's comments comparing the popularity of his band with the popularity of Jesus Christ. The right wing has gone after Ozzy Osbourne, Kiss, Judas Priest, Dixie Chicks, Bruce Springsteen, etc, etc... They seem to go after everybody who isn't Kid Rock, Ted Nugent or Chachi. So cancel culture in modern times begins way back in the 1950s and just progresses outwardly over the next 70 years. Rock has been under fire for so long, that its plight became my podcast's namesake. I named my podcast *after it*. So for those who complain that we went political in Season 4 or 5...you weren't paying attention. We were always political. From day one we spoke out against any and every constraint that has tried to suppress the progress and evolution and existence of rock music. *Rock Under Fire*...one badass, liberal, democracy-driven, all-inclusive, people-have-the-power, Antifa as fuck podcast.

We've been crying rock is dead from the sidelines for almost the entire duration of rock's existence. There was a time when artists like Pete Townshend could write the words "rock is dead" into a song, and it could become a massive hit on the radio. Anyone forming an argument in the 1970s while doubting the presence of rock during that decade would have to answer to the fact that the entire landscape they saw as conquered and depleted was still dominated mostly by rock music. Even in its most vulnerable period, which doesn't really go beyond disco's brief dominance on the Billboard charts, its presence in pop culture and center-of-the- entertainment-universe status, was never threatened...especially long before people began nitpicking over genres, dividing rock into hundreds of little categories and subcategories with every little *if*, *and* or *but* determining the factors of what style of music they were listening to. Regardless of who the act was, it fell under the banner of rock. One could argue that things like punk were anti-establishment revolutions that railed against among other things, the current state of rock music. But no matter how removed from the whole scene they pretended to be, acts like the Sex Pistols and like-minded bands were still playing Chuck Berry riffs while punk's rise and fall still happened against the backdrop of rock's dominance. This dominance remained, whether we like it or not, until the mid-1990s.

Some are suspicious of the narrative that's been commonly accepted around rock as a religion dying off with Cobain. But the past 30 years of mediocrity and invisibility speaks more to the truth of that assessment. If it's to be disproven, nobody has yet dared to show any evidence to the contrary. Our underground neo-hipsters could rave all they want about the present and how great rock music still is, and how that Brooklyn band that nobody's ever heard before has done far more important work than the Beatles. They can posture all they want about how anti-establishment they are and how uncool it is to be mainstream, and how rock is better off without the mainstream.

Well then, let it be better off.

Let's play devil's advocate for a moment and suggest rock just stay on the fringe. Let it have no real and lasting impact ever again. Let it exist solely to help neo-hipsters feel superior to everyone else. Let us remain ecstatic over the fact that when it comes down to it, the only significant and memorable piece of rock music to come out of the first two decades of the twenty-first century is the guitar riff in "Seven Nation Army." This is not to suggest there aren't any good or even great bands and artists out there, nor is it an indictment of twenty-first century rock music. It's just a reminder to those who need it, that when we think of the Sixties, Seventies and Eighties, we can easily come up with at least 20 masterpiece albums of the same high stature per year, sometimes per month. The more telling question is: *Just how many rock songs or albums can we come up with from the years 2000-2023 that have been of equal praise or merit as something released from the 1950s through the 1990s?*

Short answer: zero

The last famous culture-rattling guitar riff of the Nineties was "Smells Like Teen Spirit." The next one didn't happen until 2003 in "Seven-Nation Army." Since then?

Nothing?

Zilch.

Nada.

Niente.

Not one artist...not one band...not one album...not one song to transcend generations, other than a six-note guitar riff to represent an entire 20-year period in rock music. Let's face it... "Seven Nation Army" is really the only rock moment of the twenty-first century to leave a mark on pop culture, and most people who know it don't even have a clue who Jack White is. To most people, it's just a riff you hear at sporting events and something the marching band plays at college football games. There are just as many sports fans as music fans that know it, and yet probably less than half of them know the White Stripes.

As this book goes to publication in the final quarter of 2023, I will, for the record, state my personal five favorite songs to come out of the twenty-first century so far...and only one of them are from a rock band...and at this point, I'm perfectly okay with that. Those songs would be "Machu Picchu" by The Strokes, "Man's World" by Marina, "Make Believe" by Shannon Shaw, "The Queen" by Lady Gaga and an extremely mysterious tune called "Eyes" that I found on Soundcloud in 2016. The user/artist goes by the name of ninaduche, and there is not much else we know about her. The fact that I'm a sucker for minor chords and melodies assured that the song would grab at me instantly and then haunt me for the next seven years as I wondered just who the hell this artist actually is!

All of this said, and back to the point, the most casual rock fan could name more legendary albums from 1971 alone than came out of the entire first 20 years of the new millennium. But let's take that neo-hipster approach, and in the face of it all, still try to feed people the bullshit that rock is just as relevant as it ever was. Do you buy it?

What about the concert industry? What does it tell us when the highest grossing rock acts of the century so far have been all over the age of 60? Many who suggest that rock is just as big as it ever was, often cite festivals as evidence of just how big rock still is. The fact that there are so many festivals, they say, is proof of how much rock is still out there. But to the contrary, the fact that there are so many festivals is actually evidence of just how unpopular rock has become. Most rock bands *need* those festivals in order to play to large crowds. Most of those bands will never become popular enough to get out of the clubs. And that is the difference. The majority of well-known rock bands in the twenty-first century will never set foot in a 20,000-seat arena, while the majority of well-known rock bands during the Seventies and Eighties were *all* playing 20,000-seat arenas. That is the difference regarding the *amount of people listening* to rock music now vs. then. Again, it might be some sort of hipster pride in being able to say their band rejects the mainstream and only ten people know about them, but rock in its current form will never shake up or inform pop culture again unless the mainstream has some sort of stake in it and Gen X learns to lighten up and stop directing its social rage at rock artists. Was rock and roll just a relic of the Baby Boom generation? Was it vital only as long as the Baby Boomers were vital? Did the current crushing blow against the sentiment of protest coincide with the loss of audacity, empowerment, activism and solidarity in rock music? In plain English, did Gen X's blind embracement of right wing values in the face of everything that once made them cool and influential castrate the future of rock and roll? Did conservatives finally kill rock music like it set out to from day one? Well, even that is a little far-fetched on its own. But when we take into account Civil Rights, women's lib, gay rights, anti-war movements, the advent and popularity of Eastern spirituality, the ever-growing pushback of environmentalism, increasing numbers of kids fighting for gun control and climate change awareness, and the long road to marijuana legalization, rock and roll has been the backdrop to all of it. Unless of course rock music was merely just the art form that happened to accompany such a 50-year cultural shift to the left, and now that that shift has been fully realized and validated in terms of social progress, rock is no longer needed as hip hop has all but said "thanks, we'll take it from here." Unless of course that's true?

I've always loved that scene at the beginning of *Almost Famous* where the camera is panning over all the classic albums of the 1960s and

1970s where you start to get a sense of the canon. I think of things like this in little snapshots like romantic tirades that help me make sense of what's happened to rock music's role within the big picture. And if I can't make sense of it, I've at least been able to process these things accordingly as events that have records of themselves written in stone...somewhere. I tend to always use words like canon, much like Harold Bloom uses it to illustrate the central role of Shakespeare within the voluminous body of Western literature. But rather than look for a central figure within the rock canon, it is imperative to merely acknowledge that such a canon exists...the body of work and works, plural. The pantheon is of the gods. The canon is of their creations. The artists. The songs. The albums. The photography. The visuals and images. The legends, myths and truths. It all exists as this untouchable shrine...this palace of rock and roll...this cathedral wherein we hold sacred all that had been central, impactful and influential in the world, and therefore changed it.

But empires fall. Palaces burn. Civilizations crumble, often from within, but also due to external forces. Let's consider the downfall of the vinyl record coinciding with the downfall of rock as the central pop cultural entity. By the time hip hop, country and vocal groups took over vinyl was a thing of the past. Given the age of streaming, some of the biggest artists of the day didn't even have their product issued on CD let alone vinyl. So when we walk into a store like FYE or Barnes and Noble or any place that sells tangible music in any given shopping mall today, it is no surprise or coincidence that the majority of vinyl we see is rock music. The lifespan of the 33 1/3 record in its first incarnation was essentially the same length of time as the rock era. What is even more telling, as well as amusing, is how we can walk through a mall and be completely surrounded by the kids of Generation Z punching letters into their mobile devices...and in the middle of it all, wander into a store filled with Led Zeppelin, Rolling Stones and Beatles vinyl. It's like modern Rome surrounding the ancient ruins of the empire. This superficial excess karma of the Millennial generation, the first Internet generation, has spilled into Gen Z and is now among these ruins of yesteryear punching their way back into the culture. That said, I will stop short of suggesting that any of this will save rock. While some kids are setting their preferences to vinyl, they may very well discover layers and layers of rock that had been buried by technology and the corporate takeover of music and media. It may unfold as something unexpected in a full-circle progression, or it may be short-lived. Or as with most waves of nostalgia culture, it may just be a brief revival informed by sentimentality. Though as rock becomes less and less with each generation, so it will be with each future generation's nostalgia moment.

While civilizations may disappear due partly to those outside elements working their way inward, those civilizations leave traces of their existence. The addition of new works among the canon got fewer and farther between as we hit the 1990s, and became almost non-existent three decades into the current century. Traces remain. They always do. Ever notice that every time rock critics and fans alike go crazy over bands like the Strokes, the Hives, the Struts, Rival Sons or Greta Van Fleet, it's because they have a sound, look and style that harkens back to a time when rock was culturally relevant, and not because it's groundbreaking or original? Those unwilling to accept the manner in which history works often mistake those traces for a continuation and evolution of something they feel never ended. But the evidence surrounding the ruins tells us otherwise. If a culture looking backwards is stagnant and rock has been looking backwards for 20-plus years, then nothing has continued in the name of evolution. Nothing groundbreaking...nothing shocking...nothing...

Nothing.

But the traces do exist. They exist among what is *non*-existent, and that is the ability to make a cultural impact and influence the present as well as the future...and that has not happened with a single piece of rock music in the twenty-first century...yet. There is no shortage of new rock out there. Some of it is very good, while most if not all of it looks backwards out of necessity. And for those of us riding our nostalgia wave...well, we can see those traces and still hear the echoes of something that was much bigger than us...something louder than life. And life is pretty fucking loud before the silence happens. For now, I can't help but think of that line on the horizon behind that vast sea of emptiness where an army of young hands are raised to the skies. People reaching out in the same desperate conviction and thirst for purity as what was once handed down to them. And there are those who are brave enough to scream through the silence. But even as they scream, they're now kept on mute so it doesn't seem to matter. It's like that old question of the tree falling in the forest but nobody being around to hear it. Or maybe it was all just a dream...every last bit of it...and nothing we heard and saw was real. Or perhaps a dream *within* a dream. I think of *Picnic at Hanging Rock*...Peter Weir's masterpiece...and of Anne Lambert in the role of Miranda...standing upon those rocks just moments before being compelled onward into eternal mystery. What happens when Miranda looks and motions toward the foreboding sky just before imploring her friends to look upward? Everything begins and ends at exactly the right time and place. And so, as the lights went out on Broadway, and uptown and downtown and all around...down on Main Street, from the churches to the jails, and the subways below to the silver spaceships above...something happened as the central core began to shake while the sky roared, the earth moved and the cathedral fell to the ground. Something happened.

12

ELEGIE

In my novel *The Locker Notes*, inspired by real life events, I briefly talked about the Peterstown section of Elizabeth, New Jersey where both of my parents grew up, and where I spent large chunks of my childhood. Though the chapter ultimately deals with rock music's effect on our memories, it serves as a small personal tribute to my grandparents and all of the adult relatives who lived in Elizabeth and had some sort of role in my life. Since it's my book and applies here, I'll quote freely from it.

Peterstown was also known as the Burg and was predominately Italian during the 1970s and early 1980s. Our parents grew up there, and our grandparents and much of our extended families lived there. It is a town that irradiates the vast reaches of personal recollection just as much as our hometown.

Peterstown was full of old people. It was a grandparents' town. We figured because our grandparents lived there, everybody's grandparents must live there. It was full of streets made up of houses standing closely together, most of which were without front lawns or backyards and separated only by narrow alleys. Some houses had driveways with no garage and some had a garage with no driveway. Unlike the suburb of Oakwoods, no two houses were the same. The neighborhood was much older than Oakwoods and contained a built-in sense of history about it, even if I didn't know what that history was. Every street was filled with the Italian language and there seemed to be a deli or small food store on every corner. Staple landmarks of Peterstown included DiCosmo's Italian Ice, Saraceno's Bakery, Spirito's Restaurant and St. Anthony's Church. In between were countless little stores that seemed to be frozen in a 1950s time warp, but still felt warm and welcoming. My grandfather would take me on walks and stop in to any one of the stores to pick up his daily Il Progresso. He'd buy me Tic Tacs and always had a piece of Juicy Fruit gum for me. If we went to the store on the corner of Second and Amity, the one with the big Coca Cola sign hanging over the sidewalk, I knew I'd be in for a treat because it was the only store where I could get Dynamints. Sometimes on days when he didn't feel like walking, he'd send me out to get him his newspaper and a pack of L&Ms, which I used to love opening for him because I couldn't get enough of the smell of unlit cigarettes. Then he'd scold me for holding the pack up to my nose.

Speaking of smells, there was a distinctive odor that pervaded throughout Peterstown...a chemical scent that wasn't good but wasn't necessarily foul either. It just became the air you breathed, and you didn't think too much about it. I imagined it as a combination of paint and coffee. In reality, it was the characteristic symptoms of existing in the shadow of the Bayway refinery, which itself sat in the middle of a large industrial wasteland that haunted Exit 13 of the New Jersey Turnpike. There was also the overpowering presence of the Tenco plant in nearby Linden on the opposite side of Route 1. The smell of Peterstown couldn't be traced to any one direct culprit, but the conglomeration of scents was unique. Days were also highlighted by trips to the open-air outdoor market which took up entire blocks on the outskirts of Peterstown...vendors selling fresh fruits and vegetables amidst an unmistakably pleasant sense of Old World community, fellowship, kinship and an unspoken feeling of age-old wisdom that accompanied the entire experience.

My grandfather, Carmelo D'Errico came to America in 1956 from Monteverde, a small village in the Avellino province of Southern Italy, characterized physically by a rocky surface and sprawling hills overlooking the Campania Apennines. He took with him the same determination that so many people arrived with, though he may not have initially thought much of the so-called new world, coming from a country so rich in history and culture, and a region, that though as I've never been there, seems to have remained exactly the way it was, despite all of its modernization and renovative tweaking in recent decades. Monteverde, also the town where my dad spent the first 13 years of his life, transcended the limitations of historical timeline that we as Americans come to know as a country less than three hundred years old. There is not much of that timeline behind us, whereas Monteverde threads its story all the way back to the Lombards, at least. America could hardly have impressed my grandfather at the outset when he arrived with his oldest child Teresa who would accompany him on the start of his journey of building a new life for his family... the rest of which, his oldest son Michael (my dad), younger daughter Silvana and youngest child, Armando, remained in Italy with their mother, Maria Rosa for an additional year or two. This was the way families did it...one step at a time. While part of that American myth suggests that we take care of our own, families have to make it happen for themselves much more than any government here is going to hand anybody anything...especially when we still have one political party that acts as though it gets to decide who are Americans and who are not, while they conveniently forget that everybody has someone in their family if not themselves who at one time or another came here from someplace else to literally start from zero. My grandfather took his family to America on the strength of his will and the substance of his vision. He built a home and made a life and saw his family flourish over the course of America's most prosperous and progressive decades. His children were Baby Boomers who got to witness Elvis Presley, the Beatles and the Four Seasons in real time. His grandchildren witnessed the Bicentennial, saw the original Star Wars in the theater, rocked out to Kiss and heavy metal, stood on line to buy *Pac Man* for the Atari 2600, and belonged to the generation that helped elect America's first Baby Boom president and first black president. My grandfather's time in America spans the peak decades of modern pop culture and the lifespan of rock and roll itself.

My memories of my grandfather are multi-layered, but always initially begin with his physical attributes like his unmistakably big, boomy voice, slightly gravelly from years of smoking. He was a dignified man who always projected an unflinching aura of strength and decency. He dressed impeccably well every single day of his life...even if it was just to walk down the street for a newspaper he always wore dress pants, a suit jacket and a Fedora hat. The man had class. What I remember most about him physically is his smile and his hands. His hands were always enormous to me...both as a kid and even as I grew into an adult. Whether his hands were gripping a steering wheel or shuffling a deck of Briscola cards, they always seemed massive in their movement. I picture him mostly seated at the head of the table...

eating, drinking coffee, smoking a cigarette, reading the newspaper, playing Briscola, cutting up a chunk of provolone cheese with a loaf of Italian bread the size of a baseball bat next to it...seated at the head of the table, slicing off one piece of provolone at a time and bringing it still on the knife to his mouth...his grandson close by, watching him in all his Olympian wonder as he chewed, stared straight ahead lost in thought...looking toward the china cabinet and living room furniture containing framed photographs of all of his children and grandchildren...seated at the head of the table...always the head of the table...in slow, measured, quiet confidence like the family patriarch that he was.

When we all learned as a family that my grandfather was terminally ill, it almost didn't seem real. The news of his illness seemed to be just words at first...maybe it was denial on my part. *This situation isn't really going to happen. He's going to have treatment and he's going to be okay.*

The news came periodically over a run of 18 months. In fact, it was on my thirtieth birthday, May 9, 2000 when I was first told by my parents that he had cancer. For a few weeks into that news, he seemed fine, with not much out of the ordinary, at least on the surface. Over the course of the next year, he went through radiation and all of the treatments his doctor thought he could handle. And for a brief period, things seemed as if they'd be okay. In my life, things always ended up okay. Through my entire childhood straight up to high school graduation, they told me I was going to fail. They told me I was going to stay back and that I'd never graduate. And in the end, I'd pass. In the end, it was okay. When I got really sick twice in my mid to late-twenties, meaning "bed-ridden for months / what's wrong with him" sick, and doctors ran me through entire batteries of testing, it was always okay in the end. I didn't die like I always thought I was going to...and I got to live my life, compromised by paralyzing anxiety as it's been. I was raised and probably inadvertently conditioned to believe there was some invisible failsafe presence at work that always intervened to make things okay in the end. Some people may call that God. Maybe in my case, it's been the pure luck and luxury of having everything fall into place for so long, that when reality hits, it slams you off course into areas you'd never thought you'd encounter. And so, our family, which had been fortunate enough to remain intact in the best of health through decade after decade, was facing a new reality that had eluded us for so long. For the first time, there was going to be a death in the family.

It's not going to be okay...is it.

During the Christmas holidays of 2001, the entire family...aunts, uncles, cousins...took vigil at my Aunt Teresa's house as my grandfather's condition deteriorated more rapidly than we could have ever imagined. Bone cancer had literally eaten his physical structure away as he seemingly shrunk over a period of weeks. On the last Friday of the year, I went to my aunt's house in the mid-afternoon. Without much planning in the way family members were in and out of the house that week, it seemed as though we were there in shifts with people coming in and people going out. As I got there, my dad who'd been there all week was headed home to take a shower and get a few hours of sleep. He'd return that night. It was December 28, and I had taken my last few sick days from work as I did every year. These were the days I usually took off for the annual year-end Patti Smith shows. This year was completely out, and given the immediacy of the situation, I hadn't even thought about them until Eric called me that morning to see who was driving to the Asbury Park show. I told him I wasn't doing the Patti shows and to see if he could find someone who would take my tickets for Asbury and the Bowery Ballroom.

When I got to my aunt's house that afternoon, it was just me and my cousin Mary, alone with our grandparents. The four of us were watching the TV news which was still running 24/7 coverage of ground zero aftermath from the 9/11 attacks, along with reports from the war in Afghanistan. In his last few days, my grandfather had physically shrunk into such a slouched-over shape, that his body appeared to be curled into a ball while sitting on the couch. He could barely lift his head anymore when he called out to us that he needed to use the bathroom. Upon hearing this, I froze, because at no time in my life was I ever faced with my grandfather being this helpless, nor was he ever in a position where he needed such assistance. Instincts kick in though, and I immediately rose from my chair to help him up. I lifted him by his arms as he held on to me. I walked directly behind with my hands supporting him as we got to the bathroom, which fortunately was only about six feet from the couch. Inside, he broke away from me as if conjuring up any possible strength he may have had left...and shooed me away.

"Get out," he said laboriously.

At that moment, it hit me how surreal it all was...my grandfather... so enormous to me as a kid...so proud and majestic in presence and spirit...a man of such strength in my eyes for an entire lifetime...and here I was...holding him up. The indignity he must have felt.

The next morning, he was condemned to a bed and a catheter. Overnight, he had gotten so bad that standing up was no longer a possibility. Stubborn as he was, my grandfather protested. He still had his mind. He still had his mental faculties which were always present though most of the time his eyes were closed and it was becoming clear that he was drifting off into some other form of energy...catching glimpses of it...perhaps making peace with it. A visiting nurse informed us from her experience that he was close to passing. As Saturday, December 29 progressed, more and more of the family showed up. Halfway through the afternoon, I called Eric from my aunt's kitchen. At the time, I didn't have a cell phone yet. Eric couldn't get rid of any of the Patti Smith tickets, pretty much because everyone in our circle was already going. I hung up, deciding to eat the tickets. It wasn't important and it was nothing I could be bothered with. As I placed the phone back on the hook, my mom, being her ever-inquisitive self asked me who I was talking to and what about. Yes, I was 31 and still being pressed like an adolescent. She said I should go to the concert. I told her I was staying put and it wasn't up for debate.

"But you paid for those tickets."

"Yeah, and?"

"You have to go. Don't waste them."

"I don't care about the tickets or the money. I'm here and I'm staying here."

"Michael, you've been here all week. Go have a good time and get out of here for a while."

"Everybody is here and this is where I'm staying, now stop!"

Then my dad cut in.

"Go where you gotta go."

"No, I'm staying here. I've seen a million of these things and I don't need to be there right now."

"You've been here all week. There's nothing you can do. Go to the concert."

"The family is here, and this is where I'm staying."

As darkness fell in the late afternoon, I sat in my aunt's living room with my cousins. I remember looking around at the lights and the blackness outside the windows. Because I didn't go to my aunt's house that often, the scene reminded me of Christmas Eve and all of those past holidays of years gone by. It was a room that I associated with Christmas time. The room and the lighting looked the same, and it briefly...just for a moment...gave me the warm feeling of childhood and the way I used to feel at the start of Christmas Eve as the family were all arriving one at a time. The doorbell would ring. Who was it going to be next? The anticipation of who'd walk through the door. They'd hang up their coats in the closet and proceed up the stairs onto the landing that served as the entrance to the living room. All the while my aunt would still be preparing dinner in the kitchen and Christmas music would be playing in what was known as the family room. All the kids would gather round the table in front of the couch, usually sitting on the floor picking from whatever plates were arranged there with cheese, crackers and cookies. One of us would inevitably be seated at the upright piano. Between me and my brother, it was usually a case of who got there first. Growing up as kids, when we went to a relative's house, we'd naturally gravitate toward the things we didn't have in our own houses. When my cousins Angela, Mary and Peter would come over in the early 1980s, cable TV hadn't yet reached their section of Elizabeth, so they didn't have MTV, which meant upon entering our house, they'd automatically go downstairs and turn on MTV. When we went to their house, my brother and I would run toward the piano. Now, looking around this familiar living room where the nighttime lighting triggered a fond sentimentality, I was quickly thrust back into reality when I saw the pensive expressions on everyone's faces...all lost in their own thoughts as the room got painfully silent at times, and then suddenly my dad was shaking me back out of my own thoughts.

"Go ahead, get out of here," he ordered, still insisting I go to the concert. My mom's ears detected it and she used that as a cue to come back into the room and literally start ushering me out.

"Michael, go with your friends. Go have a good time. There's nothing you can do here. Grandpa knows you're here and he knows you've been here all week. He loves you."

On the way to Asbury Park, I had Eric and his girlfriend Jen in the car with me. They asked how my grandfather was doing, and I told them not good. As I drove to the concert, I kept replaying my last encounter with him as I said goodbye. I had taken his hand as he lay in the bed, seemingly unconscious though he was wide awake. His eyes remained closed as I kissed him and told him I'd see him later. In Italian he muttered through labored breathing that he wanted ice cream. I don't remember who said what, but as I was walking out of the room, several family members were amused that he wanted ice cream...and that was what I held on to in my immediate feeling of guilt. It was a good sign that he wanted ice cream. It meant something good. That's what I told myself.

At the Stone Pony, we got up front and center, literally against the stage. The first thing I noticed was the addition of keyboards. Ever since Patti's return to performing six years earlier, I'd only seen keyboards onstage one or two other times, and that was during the premier of the *Gung Ho* album and the first *Gung Ho* shows when she was doing a song called "Persuasion"...something she had since stopped playing. Would she be bringing it back?

As the band walked onstage, Patti was carrying a straw basket of rose petals that she tossed in the air like glitter. When she placed the basket down, Jen grabbed it. Later in the night, she'd take it with her. Jen was pretty impulsive that way and often made you fear what she was going to do next, especially when she was drunk. I likened her to a Greek maenad for the Bacchanalian frenzy she was always in...dancing, spinning...always full of excess energy, accented endearingly by an otherwise annoying hyperventilating speech that always made her sound like she had just run a marathon and was out of breath. Anyway, what I found pretty cosmic that night, was that the band opened with "Ask the Angels," the very first song on *Radio Ethiopia* which was the first Patti Smith album I ever got. Before I ever heard a note of *Horses*, it was *Radio E* that ripped me wide open and remained my favorite Patti album. I'd like to say that this song and the rose petals and stolen basket were the things I remember most about this night, but unfortunately they're not. As the show ran most of its course, the lonely keyboards on the side of the drums remained untouched. As Patti and the band got near the end of their set, bassist, Tony Shanahan sat down at the keyboards and the lights dimmed. What came next shook me to my core.

Patti stood at the mic under a lone spotlight as Tony began the opening chords of something dreadfully familiar, though it took a few seconds before I was sure what was happening. And then it became clear. They were playing "Elegie." With Patti six feet from my face, I glanced upward into empty space and closed my eyes... and I knew right then that my grandfather had passed.

Naturally, I felt a lot of guilt in the months following my grandfather's passing. I quietly beat myself up over the fact that I was the only one in the family to not be there when it happened. I was never at any point okay with being at that concert, and I wasn't at peace for a long time after it...knowing I hadn't taken control of my own circumstances and allowing myself once again to let my parents have the final word after my mom permitted my dismissal from the situation as if it were some inconvenience for me. A lifetime of this kind of conditioning wears you down and teaches you to give up, submit and obey just to keep the peace. But there's never any peace when you do that. I struggled with that one for years.

On the morning of my thirty-third birthday some sixteen months later, I woke up from a dream. In the dream, my entire family was sitting around the dining room table in my parent's house. The table was extra long with both wooden extensions locked in place...the ones that we always used for holidays when everyone was coming over. I don't know what holiday it was in the dream, or what the occasion was. Everyone was there...my parents and brother, my grandparents, aunts, uncles, cousins...everyone seated around the table with food, plates, forks, spoons, knives, glasses and bottles loosely spread around as if we had been there for hours. Everyone was lost in conversation, thought not collectively...there were many different discussions taking place at once. It was that point of the dinner when we've probably already had dessert and the kids are running around the house and nobody is required to be at the table...yet most of us were still in place. I know I was, as I sat in my usual spot in the middle of the table on the side of the dining room wall behind the kitchen. I always sat with my mom on the left of me and usually one of my cousins on my right. At the heads of the table were my dad on one end and my grandfather on the other end. In the dream however, my grandfather wasn't in his spot at the head of the table...he was sitting to my right...right next to me. What was peculiar about this was that in all my years, I don't remember my grandfather ever sitting somewhere in the middle of the table...he was always at the head. That's how I picture and remember my grandfather...at the head of the table...head of the table, head of the table, head of the table...always at the head of the table. And so, in this dream, while the entire family was engaged in various forms of talk, my grandfather and I were the only two who were not. Instead, I sat there quietly with my grandfather who was looking at me contentedly, smiling...and holding my hand.

I carried that dream around with me for the next few weeks, trying to take it apart and figure out what it meant. I've never been one for analyzing my dreams or even paying much attention to them...but this one bothered me and ate away at me. One of those dreams, as we say, that were "so real."

At the end of that month...May 2003, I went into the city with Jen who had previously mentioned that the Off-Broadway run of *Salome*, a pretty high-priced show starring Al Pacino and Marisa Tomei was selling $35 seats to a limited number of college students each day. All you had to do was show up at the box office at 9 AM and purchase your reduced tickets with a college ID. Jen had a theater background and had attended one of those New York City dramatic arts schools, but had recently started going to Rutgers and was pursuing a double major in English and Italian. I had recently gone back to county college and was ready to transfer to a four-year school after making a decision to finally get my shit together. I didn't want to live and die in the piss factory, so when I turned 30 I decided to do it for real. Back when Eric and Jen were an item, we were always hanging out in the city...usually Eric and me, after dropping Jen off at some play rehearsal, we'd roam around uptown at the Metropolitan Museum of Art or Central Park or back downtown in the Village. Sometimes we'd meet Sal for lunch or dinner in between. Now seasoned adults, we were a far cry from those teenagers who got out of the Datsun B-210 on the corner of Sixth Avenue and West Eighth in 1989. Eric and Jen had broken up, but Jen kept calling me to hang out. The common thread was always New York City, so anyone who knew they could get a ride from me, always called. It wasn't just Jen, it was everybody. It was well-known that I usually spent Friday and Saturday nights in the city and very often, at least one weeknight...so for years I became everyone's cabbie.

It was a clear and comfortable late spring Friday evening when Jen and I took a cab downtown after watching a production of *Salome*.

With our student tickets we were able to score some great seats up front and center...so close to Al Pacino that you could literally see the spit flying out of his mouth during his signature screaming scenes. We got out of the cab at Seventh and Bleecker and walked east to MacDougal. These were the last days of the four corners of Bleecker/MacDougal's radiant glory when coffeehouses marked each spot. My personal favorite, Café Borgia was the first to go when it suddenly closed without warning in January 2001 when the landlord imposed an unaffordable rent hike on the owners. The remaining three corner cafes (Café Figaro, MacDougal Diner and Carpo's) were still in business in 2003. Carpo's was once the San Remo during the days of the Beat poets. That was the one that I frequented the least of the corner cafes...not for any particular reason, but I just didn't hang out there nearly as much as the other places. Borgia had been my main hangout spot, and anyone who went into the city with me at one time or another ended up having an espresso or cappuccino there. The place hadn't undergone any interior renovations since the days when Jack Kerouac, Allen Ginsberg, Andy Warhol and Joan Baez were hanging out, so the medieval décor, marble tables and wrought-iron chairs were exactly the same through the decades. Though the original Café Borgia more times than not was my number one go-to place, Caffé Dante, a few doors south on MacDougal was also a regular haunt for me. Dante sat midblock directly across the street from the apartment where Bob Dylan lived in his post-Woodstock years. It was another establishment that existed in a time warp, much like most of the coffeehouses of the Village along MacDougal. Everything in Dante was black, white and beige. Black and white photographs of old Italy adorned the walls with black and white checker board flooring and two barred windows on the left side of the room (the non-smoking section) overlooking an alley, the side of another building, and not much view except for the backs of air conditioners. In fact, my favorite table was located right in front of one of the windows...nestled in a cozy little corner, the window just to the side and a roaring AC just above it. I spent hours at that table for years. Much of *The Locker Notes* was written there. When I walked in with Jen that night, I was mildly disappointed to see out of the corner of my eyes that two people were sitting at my table, along with the entire café being packed. We didn't even wait for the hostess to seat us. We both noticed the one empty table in the back, so we instinctively plowed through the cafe with our heads down until we reached it. For a Friday night in the Village, we were lucky to get that table without having to wait for it, so we grabbed it before anyone else did.

"Are ya mad cause your table is taken?" Jen teased.

Taking a menu from the waitress, I smiled.

"Yeah, get out of my seat!" I yelled playfully, loud enough for only the people at the table next to us to hear. My favorite table, which wasn't really visible from where we were sitting wasn't even within earshot. I looked at the menu methodically and habitually, just going through the motions, knowing already what I wanted.

Over the course of the next few minutes I must have zoned out, staring somewhere between the menu and the table...staring but not seeing...until I was disrupted by Jen's hand waving in front of my face.

"Hellooooo...Earth to Mike."

It was weird that she was trying to get my attention. Notorious for being in a perpetual self-absorbed state, getting Jen's attention was more often than not the task of everyone else. But on this particular occasion, she hadn't been drinking, and her increasing intoxication wasn't a threat. Still, I liked Jen and always saw the value of her place within our circle of friends. She was a great artist, a captivating actress, and far more ambitious than I ever was. Yet, between the unpredictable whims, the obnoxious surplus of physical and verbal energy and the drunkenness, her presence usually gave me anxiety and I was always glad she was Eric's problem to deal with and not mine. Eventually, Jen would cause more problems for me than her brand of friendship was worth and we'd never see each other again... but if there's one thing I took from her that's lasted all these years, it's the perspective she offered on a night when I needed something to pull me through the mental abyss I'd found myself in. So, as we sat at there waiting for our coffee, I decided to approach what was weighing on me.

"Let me ask your opinion on this."

Jen looked at me with one of her signature expressions...a furrowed, raised eyebrow look of concern, but overly exaggerated to the point where you had to wonder if she was acting or sincere.

"Okaaaaaayyy?" she said curiously.

Why was I even going here?

"So, I had this dream a few weeks ago..."

And I began telling her the dream about my grandfather. She had known all along how I felt guilty about not being there when he passed away. That much I made clear on the way to the Patti concert that night, even as we drove there, not fully knowing if he would still be around in the morning...I expressed to my friends that I didn't feel right leaving my aunt's house that night. That much, Jen already knew. So I told her about the dream, and how my grandfather always sat at the head of the table...and in the dream he was sitting somewhere in the middle right next to me...and how everyone's conversation somehow got filtered out and it was just me and him...and he was looking at me and smiling and holding my hand. What did it mean?

Jen, who was always the person to see signs and symbolism in everything, gave me an intense empathic, over-the-top, furrowed-brow, sympathetic stare. She was the person who always told you there's a reason for everything.

There's a reason for everything, there's a reason for everything, there's a reason for everything. And if nothing makes sense now, one day it will.

"Mike," she said, grabbing my hand. "Don't you see?"

I didn't.

See what?

I broke away from her hand, almost defensively, and snatched my coffee, raising the cup to my mouth.

"Mike, you have to stop beating yourself up. Your grandfather came to you in a dream to tell you it's okay."

"What's okay?" I asked, placing the cup back down.

She grabbed my hand again.

"Everything. Everything's okay. Everything you feel guilty about. He loves you unconditionally. He always has... and he always will. And he's letting you know that. And he's telling you... *it's...okaaaay.*"

The final okay rang out in the soft tender tone of an adult trying to reassure a child. With my eyes welling up, I closed them and nodded. One stray tear trickled down one side of my face as I pulled my hand away again.

"Yeah," I whispered, nodding again.

And somehow I knew she was right.

Jen and I talked about all of our usual topics as we finished our coffee and desserts at Caffé Dante, just as we'd sat there so many times in various configurations of our friends. On this particular clear and warm late spring evening, it was just us and the endless conversation that went on and on in intermittent stretches that cut on and off across the late Nineties until that moment,...and all our current conversational obsessions circa 2003...life and love and art and ice cream and wine and the Cherry Lane over on Commerce and Barrow. But then she casually and matter-of-factly turned it back to Patti Smith and my grandfather.

"If you ever run into Patti again, you need to tell her about that night and "Elegie."

As much as I thought about that myself, I disagreed.

"I'm just one face in a sea of countless people she probably meets every week. I can tell her that story, and yet it's just one story in a million she's heard."

"Yes, but that's *your* story. If you had to be anywhere other than your aunt's house that night, you were in the right place. You were with Patti and her music. Symbolically, "Elegie" was the connection between Patti and you. It was like a messenger, the same way your grandfather came to comfort you in your dream."

Jen's insight here was nothing new, but I agreed.

"Yes, I *have* had that thought," I said, conceding her words as valid.

The waitress brought the bill and I took it from her before she could place it down on the table.

"Mike!" Jen shouted in a whisper.

I froze, thinking she was going to scold me for taking the bill before she could see it.

Her mouth dropped open and she stared at me for a few startled seconds.

"Patti is here," she whispered frantically.

I reached into the left pocket of my jeans for my credit card, taking out a wad of cash, my driver's license and a VISA.

"Is she?" I said with a trace of disinterest, placing everything back in my pocket except the card.

"Yes, oh my God, Mike...she's right over there in your seat. At your table."

"Yeah, she's here a lot. She lives right down the block."

"Yes, but she's here right now! Oh my god, Mike...I have to go say hi."

I leaned over the table to peek around the wall where it led into the other part of the room. The person sitting at my favorite table that I saw out of the corner of my eye and didn't pay much attention to while walking in was indeed Patti Smith. Sitting across from her was Oliver Ray. I knew they had a show the next night at a place called Basilica Hudson up near the Catskills. The show had been on our radar earlier in the week, and Jen and I had actually discussed traveling upstate to see it if we could get a few more people on board. In the end, we decided against it. Nobody was around, and Jen had been broken up with Eric, so getting the two of them in the same place was very unlikely. The whole situation had become awkward for me as Jen continued to insist on hanging out. The concert though, was out of the question. But there was Patti just a few feet away, and Jen was suddenly star struck.

"Mike, you have to tell her about "Elegie."

I was having none of it.

"No, Jen...I don't. I'm gonna go pay the bill."

"Do you think I should go say hi to her?" she asked, twirling a finger through her blondish red hair against her shoulder and growing nervous.

"Sure, why not. She's right there. You may not get this chance again. Just be cool."

I got up, walked across the café to the counter and gave my card to the girl at the register. I did a once-over on all of the same pictures hanging up by the counter...the ones I always looked at with all the celebrities who'd passed through Caffe Dante over the years...guys like Pacino and DeNiro with some of the staple waitresses who had worked there for as long as I'd gone there...the women whose names I've forgotten or never knew, but whose faces were as recognizable to me as the café itself. I glanced downward to the glass display of deserts behind the counter and the mosaic assortment of cakes, pies and pastries. Should I get something to bring back, I wondered. As I waited to sign my name on the receipt, I glanced over at Jen who was still sitting at the table, watching me anxiously. I took my receipt and handed the girl at the counter her copy. When I went back to the table, Jen got her things and walked over toward Patti. I left a cash tip and purposely waited a few seconds. Out of the corner of my eye I could see Jen approaching her. I turned around and headed out, stopping behind Jen. She already had Patti's attention and was in mid-sentence.

"...I just wanted to say hi, and say thank you for helping me find my voice."

Oliver Ray kept his face down with his forehead buried in his hands, visibly not very happy that Jen was there. But could you blame him with people like us wandering over into their space and imposing ourselves into their lives?

Patti smiled politely.

"Aww, well..." she said to Jen..."I'm sure you would have found it on your own. But thank you."

Okay, that's enough, I thought. It was time to go.

"Ready Jen?" I said, purposely loud enough for one of my rock and roll icons to hear.

Patti leaned sideways and peered around Jen's body to see me standing there. She looked at me sort of squinting. At that very instant, it really hit me that I didn't want to be standing there. I stuck two fingers up in a peace sign, smiled and nodded at her. She flashed me the same peace sign, smiled and nodded back.

"Well," Jen said, "have a great show tomorrow night, I wish I could come."

"Aww, thanks." Patti said, her face alight with a generous smile, enough to let us feel like we weren't really imposing and that she appreciates that we were some small part of her journey...even if she didn't really know us. But then again, as Richard Alpert, aka Ram Dass once said...you never really meet someone who you don't already know.

With that, we turned around and walked out the door onto MacDougal Street and back into the New York City night.

"Oh my God, Mike. I can't believe I just met Patti. Oh. My. God."

"And I can't believe it was her sitting in my seat! What kind of shit is that?"

Realistically, I knew I didn't have my name on that little table, but I had to have fun with the situation while Jen went all fangirl. Geeky as Jen was, she was allowed to. I got it and I understood. I saw Patti Smith more as an old friend than some rock star. She was an artist who I'd seen more than any other artist over the years, and shared more space and moments with than any other artist. She was always the first to say that her shows were about creating the moment...the transfer of energy among the people who made up any particular scene on any given day or night...creates the moment. And the moment comes and then it's gone, vanishing into the ether. We weren't scheduled to create a rock and roll moment that night, and so the energy was a little different. We were all just living our lives and happened to meet like ships passing in the night, and then I was out the door. Life was about these moments, and I needed to get on to the next moment.

Printed in the USA
CPSIA information can be obtained
at www.ICGtesting.com
LVHW011029120624
782914LV00016B/559

9 781735 476742